CW01457684

Published by Greengrove Press

ISBN-10 1494459760
ISBN-13 978-1-49445-976-5

A CIP catalogue record for this
work is available from the British Library.

Also available as a Kindle ebook
ISBN-13 978-1-84396-287-8

Cover design
Bill Andrews

Pre-press production
www.ebookversions.com

GOD
IN A
NUTSHELL

Rex Andrews

Greengrove Press

To see a World in a Grain of Sand
And Heaven in a Wild Flower
Hold Infinity in the palm of your hand
And Eternity in an hour.

William Blake

Foreword

Rex Andrews draws together in a lucid and wide-ranging argument what it is that holds science, ethics and religion together, and challenges all the ways in which people try to prise them apart.

Scientists, moralists and believers will all have questions about some aspects of this, no doubt, but the overall vision is a compelling one – humanist in the fullest and most positive sense, religious in a way that breaks through all sorts of stereotypes.

It is a very welcome contribution to one of the most overheated and often least understood debates in our culture.

DR. ROWAN WILLIAMS

Acknowledgements

I am deeply indebted to a wide circle of colleagues for contributing to the insights developed in this volume. Membership of the World Education Fellowship, the World Council for Curriculum and Instruction and The Gandhi Foundation; Fellowships with the School of Oriental and African Studies (SOAS) and the BBC School Broadcasting Council; involvement with UNESCO and long association and research with the University of London Institute of Education have brought me in touch with a host of helpful friends and colleagues too numerous to name.

However, I must pay special tribute to a selected few whose influence has been of exceptional value in the development of my long learning curve. Professor Tomoichi Iwata (Japan), Professor Jagdish Gundara, Marc Goldstein, Dr James Hemming, Kallolini Hazarat (President of the Gujarat Research Society, India), Abbas Baba, Dr F H Hilliard, Professor Doris Lee, Professor Denis Lawton, Maggie Ing, Dr Peter Gordon, Professor William Wall, Dr Ian Michael, Dr James Henderson, Dr Antony Weaver, Professor Robert Super (USA), Professor Kenneth Cameron, Professor Adam Curle and the Very Reverent Robert Holtby.

For recent help I must thank David Kinchin, Editor of *The Congregationalist* (and Writers Bureau adviser) and his wife and son for their thorough critique of the first draft of this book; the Quaker poet, Dr Sarah Lawson, for a subsequent welcome going-over of the text; John Ransley of ebookversions.com for patiently converting my manuscript for print and ebook format; and Dr Rowan Williams for his generous Foreword. Any mistakes that remain after their helpful criticism and support are of course, mine!

As well as to colleagues, I owe a lot to the students and schoolchildren I have taught, particularly to the 9-year-old 'guinea pigs' of Dulwich Hamlet Primary School who took part in my early research on visual aids in religious education; the Sixth Formers of Wanstead High School who generously offered me their own private 'creeds' during a religious education course; the fourth year secondary schoolgirl whose exposition introduced me to Quakerism; and the Hindu, Muslim, Taoist and Confucian Rovers and Boy Scouts I encountered as their scoutmaster during my national service in Singapore.

Further back I must thank my patient, liberal-minded parents: my father nominally Church of England and my mother with Roman Catholic leanings who actually went to a Baptist church.

Finally, I must thank my wife, Marie, for her unremitting patience and help during this book's lengthy gestation.

Contents

Preface

Why 'God in a Nutshell'? There are lots of learned books describing and denying 'God' in various degrees of complexity. This is a short one. It seeks to express in simple language the findings of a long, exciting and fruitful life of research and discovery.

Its title reminds us that 'God' can be found in a nutshell, just as in you and me and in all creation. The *kernel* in a nutshell (according to my dictionary) is 'the nucleus or essential part of anything'. That seems to be a useful start in thinking about 'God'. All the principle world religions agree that there is a power beyond ourselves that creates and sustains us. And humanists and atheists are so entranced by this power that they exert prodigious efforts to try to understand it.

If we can consider this mysterious *Power we Live By* as the essential element – the 'Highest Common Factor' – in our various religions and philosophies, it helps to unravel a lot of our current problems.

Clashing definitions and descriptions of God in a fast shrinking world make for confusion and conflict instead of the harmony they are designed to promote. People die for their particular view of god. Worse still, people kill for it. Unfortunately – despite the efforts of scientists, theologians and philosophers to analyse and define it – this *Power we Live By* remains a mystery. It might be convenient to think of it as the indefinable cosmic 'X' – a force pervading for good and ill the human condition and all the intercultural and international affairs of our species and environment.

For some seventy years – since I was a ten-year-old choirboy – I have been trying to find a simple explanation for the wonders and problems that Life has blest and pestered me with. During this last decade I have found, for my own satisfaction at least, a solution that makes some sense. I hope that you might also find it useful.

Here are some of the questions considered in this book. If they have also occurred to you, you might want to share my thoughts about them:

Why and how should we try to embrace differences about fundamental beliefs?

Why do some religious fanatics resort to acts of barbarism?

Why do we get involved in wars and clashes of religion?

Why do our various religions and philosophies need 'spring cleaning'?

How can we undertake this?

Why must we use both the left (factual) and right (creative) sides of our brain?

How can we improve our understanding of how religious language works?

How can we use scriptural texts profitably, rather than destructively?

Why are we each important in the vast cosmic scheme of things?

How can we make sense of 'god' in a suffering world?

How can we relate personally to the cosmic X?

Why and when are religious rituals useful?

How can we make our own *personal* spiritual search authentic?

If you share an interest in some of these questions, let's get started...

Introduction

Our world is in a critical state of upheaval, and many blame the problems on Religion. Richard Dawkins in *The God Delusion* and Christopher Hitchens in *God is Not Great,* together with many other humanists and atheists, believe that since Darwin's great book, *The Origin of Species,* the word 'God' is obsolete and unprofitable.

True, we see, both within and between religions, a degree of discord and violence threatening the survival of human civilization in our volatile nuclear age. So how can we combat the extreme fanaticism that discredits the name of religion and restore it to its initial purpose of harmonizing relations between humankind? How, too, can we find common ground between the faithful and the scientifically-minded who rightly fear the dangers of blind superstition and unquestioned certainties?

Much of the current debate about theology seems to revolve around the question: Are humans the creatures of a God, or is 'God' the invention of mankind? Surely *both* propositions are true. The problem is essentially one of language. Words – despite the efforts of theologians – cannot describe the God who created us; but they are abundantly used to try to describe the gods we have created.

First, the God that makes us. We are brought into being by a Power urging life-forms out of the material of our planet. Whether we call this the *Source*, the *Life Force,* the *First Cause* or *God* makes little difference: this Power produces us, gives us a spell of consciousness in the world, and then re-absorbs and recycles the elements of which we are composed. Let us call this 'X' – the 'Power we live by'.

Those who ask, 'How can such a power be a loving God?' need to realise that it is the same power enjoyed by the snake that bites us, the wasp that stings us, the germs that invade us as well as all the other species that share our planet (and possibly our cosmos) with us. So much for divine favouritism! And those who think they know the nature of God in detail need to recognize that this Power remains a total mystery to us. Science and language can study, record and exploit its effects, but its *ultimate* nature is inaccessible to limited human language.

However language, despite its limitations, gives us an astonishing advantage over the other creatures sharing our environment. While they remain blissfully unselfconscious of their nature, humans are enticed by language to *reflect* self-consciously on our existence – to ask questions like 'why?' and 'how?' which project us into the fields of philosophy, theology and ethics. This leads us on to the gods that we create. Ironically, it is with our God-given intellect and imagination that we have created the gods we worship (or reject, as the case may be) and the ethical systems that go with them.

These man-made gods, *constructed* of various elements welded together, are artistic and poetic creations. Unfortunately, with the passage of time, many people fail to recognise the symbolism, anthropomorphism and other poetic devices used in their construction, and find themselves embattled about unimportant, extraneous details. The faithful forget how committees devised their dogmas and lose touch with the Power that created them; and the sceptics look to Science for their salvation.

This book seeks to find common ground for all

concerned with our shared life on this planet; for all who regret the activities of fanatical extremists; and for all who want to promote global harmony for the sake of our children and their children's future. It proposes a concept of 'God' appropriate for the 21st century.

CHAPTER ONE

Crisis: the X of 'extremism'

> *Men never do evil so completely*
> *and cheerfully as when they do it from*
> *religious conviction.*
> Blaise Pascal, Pensees, 1670

> *In great contests each party claims to act in*
> *accordance with the will of God. Both may be, and*
> *one must be wrong. God cannot be for*
> *and against the same thing at the same time.*
> Abraham Lincoln, Memorandum, 1862

> *A faith is something you die for; a*
> *doctrine is something you kill for: there is*
> *all the difference in the world.*
> Tony Benn, The Observer, 1989

God in a Nutshell

If there is any one essential element common to all the various traditional concepts of God, I believe it can be expressed 'in a nutshell' as *'the Power we Live By'*, or (in a slightly extended form) *the power beyond ourselves that gives us, and sustains, our lives*. The nature of this power, and our relation to it is open to a wide variety of interpretations. For the sake of argument we can call this element the X Factor.

There are a number of reasons that make 'X' an appropriate symbol in this case. In the first place 'x' is used in algebra to represent an *unknown quantity* – just as for us humans, in the final analysis, the precise nature of 'God' remains a mystery. Moving to another mathematical metaphor, in geometry 'x' is 'the first coordinate', and a coordinate is *'something that brings various parts and movements into a proper relation to ensure harmony or effective operation.'* It seems to me that, ideally, this would seem to be the nature and function of the Power beyond ourselves by which we live. (Unfortunately, apart from some unavoidable, innate problems in the nature of things that will be discussed later, destructive human activity also gets in the way of this ideal all too often!) At the risk of stretching a point, maybe it is worth remembering that 'X' occurs in stories of human quests to mark 'the spot where treasure lies'! Finally, the fact that 'X' is a cross – albeit an oblique cross – reminds us of one of the religions we shall be dealing with. But it is not my purpose here to emphasize one religious quest above the others; my concern is to find and discuss the highest common factor that unites them all.

As a matter of convenience, I feel that using 'X' in an objective discussion of the divinity avoids having to use 'he' or 'she' or worse still 'it'. The image of 'God' as a male or female 'person' immediately complicates the issue. Perhaps I should point out, so as not to offend mathematicians who generally use a lower case 'x' to represent an unknown quantity, that in the present discussion I thought it more seemly to use a capital 'X'.

Our search for a common element – X – in all human constructions of God can help to establish some common ground between rival faiths (and even non-believers) and reduce some of the tensions threatening global solidarity. Although it is true that the majority of Christians, Jews,

Muslims and Humanists have shown themselves capable of peaceful co-existence despite their differences, the upsurge of fanaticism among certain elements calls for urgent action if our shared civilization is to be preserved. As passionate believers of different faiths and ideologies in our global village are thrust together by modern technology – which can either unite or destroy us – the more we understand ourselves and each other and the more we understand the way we use terms such as 'God', 'Allah', 'Yahweh' and the many other names for divinity, the better we can organize our lives for the common good. Currently we have got ourselves and our God-concepts into a tangle. Chapter 2 will seek to unravel some of the knots. Meanwhile let us see where the present drift is taking us.

Extremism and Secular Drift
It appears that in Europe belief in God is steadily waning. This is not altogether surprising when we consider the behaviour of religious extremists who justify their violent actions by reference to gods of justice, truth and love.

No doubt al-Qaida's terrorism, that has been tarnishing the name of Islam for several decades, is one of the worst offenders. A recent copy of *The Guardian Weekly* (01.02.2013) reveals that even more than a decade after the 'Twin Towers' episode, 'a frightening picture' of al-Qaida mayhem remains – including fighting in Mali and a devastating hostage-taking attack on an Algerian oil refinery. The article continues:

> In recent weeks there were arrests in the Philippines, anti-terrorist operations in Indonesia, deaths in Pakistan, air raids in Afghanistan on suspected al-Qaida bases, battles in the Yemen, shootings and executions in Iraq following the

release of a video showing brutal executions... [and] reports of trials in the UK and Germany.

Apart from Islamist jihadists and the Taliban enforcing strict, ruthless *sharia* law on unwilling populations, other violence associated with religious extremism takes a variety of forms. Hindus and Muslims clash on the borders of India and Pakistan; Christians are molested by the government in largely Buddhist Myanmar; Muslims and Israelis are continually embattled in the Middle East; and even – still – occasional clashes occur between Protestants and Catholics in Northern Ireland. Of course, these religious conflicts are interwoven with political issues, but the faith element tends to heighten the emotional commitment of the opponents.

There is nothing new about this kind of news. Unsurprisingly, a *Guardian* ICM poll some six years ago (December, 2006) found 'more people in Britain think that religion causes harm than believe it does good.' Only 33% of those questioned in the same poll would 'describe themselves as a religious person' and 82% said 'they saw religion as a cause of division and tension between people.'

More recently, an IPSOS Social Research poll (April, 2011) revealed that the proportion of the populations who 'did not believe in God or a Supreme Being' was 34% in Great Britain, 31% in Germany and 39% in France. Even in America a Gallup poll (June 2011) shows a small drop in belief in God across the population to 92%, (90% among younger Americans) compared with a fairly constant figure of 98% throughout most of the second half of the twentieth century. (Worldwide, meanwhile, the same IPSOS poll shows that, globally, 'definitive belief in a God or Spiritual Being' is at about 51%, – ranging from 93% in Indonesia to 10% in Russia.)

What exactly is 'a religious person'? A poll in France

since the turn of this century revealed some interesting figures. Of 51% of respondents claiming to be Catholics only 17% were regular churchgoers, and only 26% of the professed French Catholics felt certain of the existence of God. A further 26% thought it was 'probable'. It was also interesting that of the 52% believers or 'probables' 79% thought of God as 'a force, energy or spirit' rather than an entity 'with whom one can have a personal relation'.

The drift from orthodoxy towards a consideration of a more rational religion is dramatically illustrated by two women writers, Karen Armstrong and Ayaan Hirsi Ali. They are both refugees from situations of intense devotion rather than extremism. Karen Armstrong finally abandoned her life as a nun after seven years in a convent. In *The Spiral Staircase* she recounts the spiritual process that led to her rejection of the Christian nuns' habit.

In a parallel autobiography, entitled *Infidel,* Ayaan Hirsi Ali tells of her reasons for finally abandoning the Muslim burka. Both, however, recognize the fact that religion will not go away. Karen Armstrong admits to a yearning for 'the infinite and ultimately satisfying mystery that we call God' but she is disturbed by the excessive certainty shown by the dogmatic faithful in the absence of detailed evidence. In her view: 'Maybe this is the time for honest, searching doubt, repentance, and a yearning for holiness in a world that has losts its bearings.' She believes that, if our concepts of God are to serve our life on earth and not destroy it, we need a more critical understanding of our faiths. To this end, in her view 'the study of other people's beliefs is now no longer merely desirable, but is necessary for our very survival'. Hirsi Ali, in her turn, recognizes that Islam 'is in a period of transition, that the religion as it is currently practiced is often incompatible with modernity and democracy and must radically transform itself' (*Guardian Weekly* 2-8/3/2007). Her particular motivation in adopting this move 'from the world of faith to the world of reason' is the need to promote fuller respect for the role of women and concern for their welfare.

Among scientists, Stephen Hawking, the renowned physicist who had until recently retained a shadowy place for God, decided in his latest book, *The Grand Design* (Bantam, 2010), that our current knowledge of the laws of physics 'renders the idea of divine intervention redundant'. Previously, in *A Brief History of Time*, he had suggested that when we have a complete theory to explain the universe 'we should know the mind of God'. Now he states that to set off the Big Bang, 'it is not necessary to invoke God to light the blue touch paper'.

It is not surprising, in view of the disarray, contentiousness and current resurgence of violence in the name of religion that the atheist Stephen Hawking can distance himself from religion and Richard Dawkins, can have a field day at the expense of the 'faithful'. Dawkins' book, *The God Delusion,* although heavily one-sided in its argument, is otherwise serious, well researched and a timely wake up call to counteract the extremism in the various faiths that is currently leading us into the mire.

Apparently, however, Dawkins' main concern is that most current *notions* of God are delusions, since it seems to me that he is mostly arguing about questionable propositions that are continually promoted *about* God. His main attack is directed against *organized religion* and blind, unquestioning acceptance of its dogmas by adherents. His championship of science is virtually 'religious' in its fervor, yet he overlooks the fact that there is a great need for a spiritual element in life. He also forgets the positive elements and achievements of religion – the social cohesion it offers; countless examples of personal sacrifice; the creation of beautiful buildings, art works, music and so on; and the way religions offer models to live up to, as opposed to abstract calculations. Paradoxically, the values underlying Dawkins' argument are essentially the Christian values of compassion and justice that the church with all its faults has transmitted from one generation to another.

In rejecting 'divine *intervention*', Stephen Hawking's recent book dismisses a conception of divinity that is irrelevant to the God of the X factor, the subject of the present book. The concept of god I am proposing is far from being an 'interventionist god' or a 'god of the gaps', but is much closer to the all-embracing God expounded by Spinoza. But more of this in later chapters.

The main problem with Dawkins' and Hawking's approach is their failure to recognize that religion will not go away. If they could start from scratch the situation might be different. But the fact is that millions are born into faith environments that most are psychologically and emotionally unwilling or incapable of surrendering. It is highly unlikely that they will all readily surrender their churches, mosques, temples and synagogues in favour of scientific rationalism.

Ironically, a curious overall trend appears to bear this out. Speaking at the Royal Society of Arts in London (15 April 2010) Eric Kaufmann, Reader in Politics at Birkbeck College, University of London, pointed out that; 'far from declining, religious populations are actually multiplying, and this extraordinary demographic phenomenon indicates that the more religious people are, the more children they will have.'

Unlike the ultra-humanists' lobby, Kaufmann is not alarmed by this trend. As a utilitarian, he believes that 'the maximization of collective happiness is the proper end of humanity; and on that score, religion seems more rational than irreligion'

In an article 'Shall the Religious Inherit the Earth' (*The Independent*, 9 April 2010) the reviewer, Ziauddin Sardar, summarises Kaufmann's thesis:

> All the evidence of recent happiness research suggests that people who believe in God are far happier than atheists. This is equally true of individuals as of nations...For the world's poor, religion is not just a source of meaning, identity and happiness; it is also a symbol of resistance. It points towards alternative possibilities beyond the greed, materialism and arrogance of secular societies. Those who believe that science, art, humanism, or a 'love of life in this world' can replace God are totally removed from the overriding concerns of the rest of the world.

This would suggest that belief in God, regardless of their concept of God's nature, is a positive element contributing to the happiness and fulfilment of the lives of many. It is close to the view prefigured by the sociologist, Emile Durkheim, nearly a century ago, in *The Elementary Forms of the Religious Life* (1915). Although approaching religion as a scientist, Durkheim recognised religion as both a necessary and somewhat mysterious aspect of human behaviour and aspirations. He summed up his extensive research with a similarly positive attitude towards the contribution of religion to social well-being. He concluded that 'all the great institutions have been born in religion...because the idea of society is the soul of religion' (pp.418-19).

Religion, he believed, was a striving for a perfect society. We have to recognise that Society

...is not an empirical act, definite and observable; it is a fancy, a dream with which men have lightened their sufferings, but in which they have never really lived. It is merely an idea which comes to express our more or less obscure aspirations towards the good, the beautiful and the ideal. (p.420)

Durkheim believed that these aspirations were innate, and that the ideal society depended on mankind's religious instinct rather than being responsible for it.

Extravagant Religion

Concepts of God, in a multitude of guises, have a long history. Any attempt to jettison the idea of divinity for the future is a non-starter. Our problems arise not because the word 'God' (and its various translations) exists, but because of the way it is used. There is still value in the word 'God': my misgivings are about the way the word is bandied about, the excessive weight of 'baggage'that it is obliged to carry, and (most of all) what it is used by extremists to justify. Despite these problems, I don't belong to the 'death of God' or the 'delusion of God'school. We do need, however, to give some thought to some of the mind-boggling delusions *about* God entertained by both believers and their opponents.

Unfortunately, the world is too dangerous now to allow for luxuries of fantasizing and wishful thinking among the 'extravagantly faithful'. Although the majority of the vast number of religiously minded individuals in the world are no doubt decent citizens, playing a responsible part in their various communities, there is unfortunately a dangerous minority of zealots in every faith group. There is, for example, a significant number of Christians eager for an Armageddon so that they can enjoy the so-called 'Rapture' of the chosen and the suffering of the rejected. And there is a disturbing body of fanatical Islamists ready to take a short cut to paradise through martyrdom by blowing themselves up in crowded market places. Neither bring much credit to their faith nor show much respect to their faith's founders. The more moderate and thoughtful Christians, Muslims and others watch these antics in horror, unable to calm their over-zealous fellows and restrain them from their excesses.

Since the events of 9/11 the more enlightened believers deplore the ways their respective faiths have been exploited. Where, they ask, was the compassionate and merciful Allah of Islam in the horror of the Twin Towers episode? Where was the loving God of Christianity in the disgraceful use of torture in the Abu Ghraib and Guantanamo prisons sanctioned in Iraq by the supposedly God-fearing western powers? And where was the just God of Judaism in the Israeli assault on Lebanon and in the current stranglehold on their neighbouring Palestinian population? These examples may vary in degree and in the weight of the political dimension involved, but there is no doubt that a religious element plays a significant part in all three,

It is arguable that whatever 'faiths' some people profess, their real 'gods' are power, money, oil, personal (rather than general) salvation, nuclear bombs, sex and celebrities, since these are the issues which mostly consume their resources and attention. It was not happenstance that made the Twin Towers and the Pentagon the victims of Islamist extremism on September 11th 2001. The once 'almighty dollar' and NATO's 'nuclear-powered hypocrisy' were obvious symbols to arouse Islamic disapproval. Another source of contention between Islam and the West is their unhealthy preoccupation with sex – Islam hiding it and the West flaunting it. There is no separating these materialistic issues from religion. Each faith, with its various concepts of God, clearly has much to say on power, sex and spending.

The second decade of the twenty-first century finds extremist religious views flourishing on the world-wide web promoting religious and racial hatred in fifteen monitored countries including the UK and the USA. Wherever they come from, these fanatical mavericks use their websites in an attempt to destroy good relation between more enlightened Christian, Islamist, Judaic, humanist and other individuals and communities. With or without encouragement from the web, extremist activities are reported daily by our news media. Some typical examples:

*   In Islamabad: 'The governor of the state of Punjab was assassinated by one of his own bodyguards...(because he)...had recently angered Islamists by appealing for a Christian woman, sentenced to death for blasphemy to be pardoned. (*The Week, 9/1/2011*)

*   In Cairo: 'Christians rioted...in the wake of a suspected Islamist bomb attack on a Coptic church...in which twenty-three worshippers were killed. The interior ministry blamed "foreign elements" for the bombing at the Saints Church, which had been named as a target on an al-Qa'eda affiliated website.' (*The Week, 9/1/11*)

*   In North America: 'anti-abortionists have killed nine people in the past two decades and are responsible for between 10,000 and 15,000 violent actions.' (*Financial Times, 6/9/2010*)

*   In Afghanistan, for a long period, numerous areas were 'without girls schools, due to attacks on teachers and students by the Taliban...and traditional practices such as child marriage and "baad", in which women are exchanged like objects in tribal disputes' went unchallenged. (*Guardian Weekly, 8/12/2006*).

17

* The eruption in 2011 of violent religious and cultural hatred in Norway – both on the web and in the cold-blooded murder of scores of peaceful citizens by a lone fanatic – was perhaps the least expected example.

This daily reported destructive and irrational behaviour typifies the extravagant lengths many misguided and fanatical believers will go to in order to prove their devotion to their beliefs.

A Changing World

Our world has changed radically since the great religions were founded. Consequently a more rational understanding of God, based on the insights we have acquired in the interim, would provide a safer and truer anchorage for our faith-concepts today. We need to examine our beliefs and assess how they fit in with our responsibilities to the world situation as it exists now.

Those people who rightly feel that they owe their life to a power greater than themselves might be tempted to mistake this power for an irrational being – focusing on some of the more fanciful, symbolic 'trappings' of their faith without examining it critically. But just as the major religions have adapted themselves in the past to changing times and circumstances, those same faiths are still capable of modification to meet the urgent needs of the 21st Century.

Many religious leaders and theologians have a much more advanced understanding of their faith than their flocks, and some would welcome a deeper and more mature appreciation of religion from their congregations. It should not alarm Christians when an Archbishop questions the details of the traditional Nativity story, but reassure them that the church is keeping up with the 'Zeitgeist' – the spirit of the age.

Not only has our world changed over the centuries, but our understanding of the nature of these changes has altered considerably in the last century. Arguably it was not until the late eighteenth and nineteenth centuries that a true sense of historicity emerged. From a biological point of view human nature does not change substantially. But culturally, new knowledge, insights, facilities and circumstances have made significant differences to us. Each age has its own 'Time-Spirit': the furniture of our minds changes along with the furniture of our homes, and fashions in appropriate behaviour change as naturally as fashions in our clothing.

The word 'historicity', defining this phenomenon, was first coined in 1880 and soon after that the German word 'Zeitgeist' meaning 'Time-Spirit' was introduced into England by Matthew Arnold in his book *Literature and Dogma* (1884). Since then the term has proved useful to historians and others concerned to study and convey the thought and feeling peculiar to a generation or period. We are now much more aware of the fundamental disparity there can be between the thought patterns of one generation and another.

We are also more alert to the way words change their meanings not only in translation but also in response to cultural and environmental change over time.

Different times bring different needs and remedies. We would not today willingly consult a mediaeval doctor dealing in astrology, humours, random herbs and blood-sucking leeches for our body's health. And most of us would rather rely on a modern 'satnav' than a fourteenth-century map to get to our destination. Yet, for their soul's sake, many people are happy to put their trust entirely in the hands of scribes living in a total different 'Zeitgeist' many centuries or millennia ago.

Dawkins and Darwinism

To some degree Richard Dawkins is seeking to do for the
21st century what Matthew Arnold, the distinguished
educationist, poet and social critic, attempted to do in the
19th century: to rid religion and morality from unthinking
dependence on supernatural and miraculous authority.
However, Arnold wanted to rescue Christianity from these
sanctions, whereas Dawkins would be happier to abolish
religious allegiance altogether. Dawkins' more desperate,
negative and thoroughgoing approach may be explained by
the increased dangers we face today. Inter-religious
violence, Dawkins recognises, especially between extreme
Muslim and extreme Christian views, is vastly more
threatening to twentieth century stability than it was to the
nineteenth century world. After all, as Einstein claimed,
'the release of atom power has changed everything except
our way of thinking, and thus we are driven unarmed
towards catastrophe'. In Einstein's view 'The solution to
this problem lies in the heart of mankind.' This is also true
of Dawkins'view, I believe, but his writing style focuses
primarily on the 'mind' rather than the 'heart' of mankind,
and the *scientific mind*, in particular. He proposes atheistic
humanism as the only viable alternative to the various
'delusions' of God held by the different faith communities.

In order to combat some of the problems created by
religions, Richard Dawkins appears to propose a new
dogma of 'Darwinism' in opposition to the dogma of a
'Designer God'. This opposition seems to me to reflect a
misunderstanding of both concepts. I have as much
admiration for Charles Darwin's achievement as Dawkins
has. The brilliant and painstaking work that produced *The
Origin of Species* has changed and enriched our
understanding of the nature of life. Darwin's work,
however, is scientific *description*: Darwin would never

have sought to present himself as the power behind evolution. His insights were prophetic, as subsequent research is proving, but Darwin is not a sort of god-substitute. On the other hand, the concept of a 'Designer God' as imagined by many fundamentalists is simply the result of a misunderstanding of a passage of imaginative poetry in the *Old Testament* book of Genesis. By opposing scientific research to misappropriated poetry, Dawkins is confusing the issue – which is to understand the nature of the Power that inspired both the science and the poetry.

Dawkins quotes Phillip E Johnson's definition of Darwinism as 'the story of humanity's liberation from the delusion that its destiny is controlled by a power higher than itself.' I think there is a lot of truth in this. But, to avoid confusion later on, I must point out that the existence for humanity of a 'power higher than itself' does not necessarily imply that such a power is 'in control' of humanity: we can equally envisage a power that *creates* humanity, *nourishes*, *fuels* and *recharges* it. As the old German hymn goes:

> *We* plough the fields and scatter the good seed on the land,
> But it is fed and watered by *God*'s almighty hand.
> (M.*Claudius 1740-1815, translated by J.M.Campbell*)

Putting aside the anthropomorphic 'hand' of God – that immediately suggests the image of the 'bearded old man' – we have here the nub of probably all religions: a concept of humanity's existence and toil *supported* by a power beyond itself. It has to be understood that Darwin's theory of evolution equally depends upon a dynamic power that propels and supports the various living species as they emerge and flourish.

Darwin was of course a naturalist and his work on the origin of species, grounded in nature, steers clear of *super*-naturalism. Both Darwin and Dawkins, while renouncing the supernatural, 'stand in awe at the structure of the world'. Dawkins, moreover, has a good deal of sympathy for what he calls 'Einsteinian religion' – a pantheistic belief in 'Spinoza's god who reveals himself in the orderly harmony of what exists, not in a God who concerns himself with the fates and actions of human beings.'suffice to say here that despite the title of his book *The God Delusion,* Dawkins' main concern is with religions, the delusions they have *about* 'God', and the extraordinary and dangerous behaviours the extravagantly 'faithful' are led to indulge in as a result of these delusions. I have a good deal of sympathy with this; but I am far from agreeing with the idea that we should seek to abolish religions and relinquish the idea of God.

Time to Refine our Religious Concepts

My own feeling is that, given the degree of allegiance that the majority of people attach to the faith community they are born into, it is more realistic to encourage a general 'spring cleaning' of concepts within the various religions than to argue for their total abandonment. Individuals have more control over their conceptions of God than most people realize. While each religion constructs its concept of God in its own way, within these faith formulations each individual contrives his or her own *personal* God concept based on their experience, encounters, imagination and intelligence.

Much of the current debate about theology seems to revolve around the question: 'Are humans the creatures of a God, or is "God" the invention of mankind?' If we think about it, it becomes clear that both propositions are true.

22

The problem is essentially one of language. Words –
despite the efforts of theologians – cannot describe the God
who created *us*, but they are abundantly used in attempts to
describe the Gods *we* have created.

I am sure that the God I relate to won't be exactly the
same as yours, nor will yours be identical with your next-
door neighbour's, nor even your spouse's. Nor is my
conception of God like the 'God' my atheist friends quite
rightly reject – the one they were force-fed with before they
were allowed to think for themselves. It has taken me a
long time to realize that my God is a *construct* distilled
from numerous elements welded together. We have to look
at the way some of these elements come together and
entangle religious ideas so that the essential core is
obscured. The next chapter seeks to find the lost centre of
the major faiths.

CHAPTER TWO

Unravelling the X Factor

> *Every man recognizes within himself*
> *a free and rational spirit, independent of his body.*
> *This spirit is what we call God.*
> Leo Tolstoy, The Gospel in Brief, 1880

> *'When I use a word,' Humpty Dumpty*
> *said in in a rather scornful tone, 'it means*
> *just what I choose it to mean –*
> *neither more nor less.'*
> Lewis Carroll,
> Alice Through the Looking Glass, 1872

> *Man cannot make a worm,*
> *yet he will make gods by the dozen.*
> Michel de Montaigne, Essays II, 1580

The Lottery of Identity

I was eight years old when the first air raid siren of World War Two sounded and we waited for enemy aircraft to come over and unload their bombs. For the next six years we were daily urged by the 'wireless' and newspapers – to hate the Germans. Although, like loyal Britons, we joined in our own small way with the war effort, my mother reminded us that in addition to Scottish and Irish blood we also had some German ancestry not very far back. I began to wonder what it would have been like if I had been born in Berlin instead of London. What would my life be like? What would *I* be like?

From then onwards, while I despised Hitler's Nazism, I began to recognize that the average German would probably be much like myself. After the war, of course, I discovered the essential truth of this.

Later, as I sang in a local Church of England choir, I began to wonder what my ideas and my life would be like if I had been born in a Catholic or Jewish family, or (more daringly) into a Hindu, Muslim, Buddhist or atheist environment.

These thoughts gradually made me realize that we are not born Christians, Jews, Muslims, etc; we are born into a Christian, Jewish or Islamic *society*. It took considerably more time to realize that these societies were man-made – the result of the convergence and interaction of a complex range of economic, political, social and religious forces.

Meanwhile, by the time I reached adulthood I understood, like every other reasonably thoughtful person, two truths: (1) that if we had been born elsewhere we would have a different religion and life philosophy, and (2) that whatever religious or other belief we each have, we all owe our lives to precisely the same force (Creator, God, Nature – by whatever name) as each other.

Without pressing the numbers game too closely, current estimates suggest that this Power – let us call it X to save arguments – has currently facilitated the birth on this planet of some 7 billion human babies. Let us see how these are distributed in terms of the religious environments (e.g. households) to which they are nominally assigned:

Christian	2 billion
Muslim	1.5 billion
Hindu	1 billion
Buddhist	500 million
Chinese/Communist	23 million
Baha' I	5.7 million
Jains	4 million
Zoroastrian	200,000
Atheists	1 billion
Various minority religions, Agnostics and Don't Knows	967,100,000

Logic and common sense dictate that an all-wise, all-knowing and all-loving god would not create all this diversity and potential source of antagonism as part of a great plan or design – still less as a cynical game to watch while these creatures fight it out. Clearly there is something wrong with our partisan conceptions of the godhead. We need either to ditch the idea of divinity altogether as Richard Dawkins proposes, or to redefine and reconstruct a notion of God that is more generally credible – a concept that can be shared widely. Perhaps we need not be too despondent about the range and variety of religions, but regard this as a challenge. In *The Religious Experience of Mankind* (Fontana Library, 1971) Ninian Smart suggests that not only is the study of a *variety* of religions 'a fascinating and stimulating task', but: this variety (is)

> testimony to the richness of the religious sense and imagination of mankind, and often – though by no means always to the nobility of the human spirit… [and] …also gives rise to some profoundly important questions about the truth of religion. (p.12)

One of these questions I feel bound to ask is: how has it come about that so many intelligent members of the genus *homo sapiens*, looking around at the prodigious variety of faiths extant, can imagine that their own sect or persuasion is the only *true* one specially 'chosen' by their maker, and that the others are somehow inferior fakes? It would be a very unjust creator who operated such an unfair production line.

Hidden Complexities in the 'God' Concept

I agree with Dawkins that there are delusions about 'God' and approve of his search for truth in these matters. I also think that his debunking of irrationalism, hypocrisy and superstition is timely. But it is not 'God'that is the delusion: it is the accretions, paraphernalia and false ideas associated with 'God'that create the problems. William Occam, the fourteenth century English philosopher, had a way of dealing with such issues. His dictum, popularly known as 'Occam's razor', is usually translated as 'no more things should be presumed to exist than are absolutely necessary' (*Entia non sunt multiplicanda praeter necessitatem*). He clearly meant 'things' here to include concepts, ideas and trappings. But this helpful advice seems to have been largely ignored by theologians of most schools. Thanks to them the original teachings of the founders of our major religions tend to get lost among a plethora of no doubt well-meant accretions. We need to get back to the kernel of truth that is lodged somewhere among the creative excesses of the theologians throughout the centuries. I am convinced that there is a shared element – 'X' – that merits the term 'God' (or 'Allah', 'Dieu', etc) and is far from being a delusion.

God (whether regarded also as 'Creator' or 'First Cause') is for most religions primarily 'the object of worship'. But around this hub, theologians have built a whole complex of accessories.

According to Ninian Smart, a religion 'is a six-dimensional organism, typically containing (1) *doctrines, (2) myths and (3) ethical teachings,* as well as (4) *rituals,* (5) *social institutions,* and (6) *religious experiences* of various kinds' (p.31). The last three of these dimensions are essentially the behaviour and activity by which the faithful express their devotion and response to the divine. It is in the first three dimensions that the various concepts regarding 'God' become complicated. The dogmas, myths and teachings of most religions, variously incorporate miracles of resurrections, virgin births, reincarnations, divine or demonic entities and locations, rewards and punishments and so on. From the beginning of a religion throughout its life such elements may be added, modified or deleted by mutual consent (as times and circumstances change), or more usually by official dictum from the relevant guardians of authority.

Different notions of God, or of gods, have been with us for a long time. Once humankind had evolved language, and with it self-consciousness and verbal creativity, humans began to express their ideas about powers other than their own. Such powers were inevitably manifestations of the natural world on which they depended: the sun, moon, stars, rain, earth and sky being among the earliest to be named and deified. But gradually the number multiplied and increased in subtlety and complexity: gods of love, war, victory, ocean, time, wine, wisdom and so on were recognized. The Egyptians, Hindus, Greeks and Romans were particularly inventive. (Traditionally there are 330 million Hindu gods, though three of them Brahma, Visnu and Siva emerged as the most important.) Later, Judaism, Christianity and Islam rejected this polytheistic expansion

in favour of monotheism. The wording of the Mosaic Law –
'Thou shalt have no other gods *before* me' – seems to leave
a margin for other subservient gods. But Islam is adamant:
'There is no god but Allah and Muhammad is his
messenger.'

Human creativity saw to it that this was not the end of
the story. There were *already* different *kinds* of
Christianity: the Orthodox Church in the East, and in the
West, Roman Catholicism; in due time there was
Protestantism, then Seventh Day Adventism and goodness
knows how many other *'isms'*, each proclaiming a God of
a different complexion. Islam was similarly creative. While
sharing the 'One Only God' with Judaism and Christianity,
it soon conceived it differently from Shi'ite, Sunni and Sufi
perspectives. At the same time religions were burgeoning in
Africa, the Americas, the Far East and the Pacific! It is
calculated that, before the end of the twentieth century, in
the USA alone there were about 3,700 sects and religions
(Carl De Kayzer, *God Inc.*, Amsterdam, Focus, 1992), each
presumably with its own conception of God.

God-made Man and Man-made Gods

Virtually all religions and sects proclaim among other
qualities the 'goodness' of God. In English the word 'God'
is conveniently close to the word 'good'. However, despite
appearances, it seems that the English word 'God' is in fact
derived from a Teutonic word *gutho* meaning 'that which is
invoked, called upon or worshipped by sacrifice'. (The Old
Irish word *guth* – *voice* – shares the same origin.) *The
Shorter Oxford English Dictionary* defines 'god' as 'a
superhuman person... who is worshipped as having power
over nature and the fortunes of mankind; a deity', or as 'a
worshipped image or idol'. In the monotheistic sense God
is defined as 'the One object of supreme adoration; the

Creator and Ruler of the Universe'. (While the term 'object' conveniently avoids giving the divinity a gender, it seems a little flat to define a vital and omnipresent Power!)

Although all creatures (including humans) are manifestly made by a 'Power not themselves' which I believe it is convenient to call 'God', it is equally true that all the gods men worship are man-made. It is mankind who decides to call this or that concept or person a god. (I would like to be able to say '*human*kind' but in fact it seems that womenfolk are generally debarred from participating in these decisions!) Examples of this deification process include: the Sun (Apollo), or War (Mars), a winged Messenger (Mercury), or a wise and benevolent Elephant (Ganesha), etc. The Romans had a habit of creating gods out of emperors. Deification is essentially a human act. To *deify* is 'to make a god' or 'to regard or worship as a god'. Thus it was that during the Roman Empire (under Constantine the Great) at the Council of Nicea (325 c.e.) that the man Jesus was elevated into a god – or, at least, into a third of a god – when the Athanasian doctrine of the Trinity was adopted by a committee of Bishops of the Christian Church.

In one respect this was an advantage, in that it ensured that Jesus' life and message would continue to be made widely known. On the other hand, it was perhaps unfortunate because it encouraged people (or often forced them) to *worship* him instead of following his precepts. Interestingly, liberal thinkers – including many Jews and Moslems – often appreciate Jesus' life and teaching the more because they don't distance him by deification, but value his essential humanity.

Leaving this particular instance, let us now look at a range of religions to see how they view 'God' and see if we can find the HCF – the highest common factor – across the board. Is there any one attribute that we can call 'X'that is shared by all or most religions?

Origins of Deity

It is of course impossible to know exactly when the first inklings of godhead came into men's minds. The detailed evolution of humanity from its primitive beginnings is essentially a closed book, leaving many such tantalizing questions unanswerable. Clearly the concept of a 'god' depended on the development of speech, but it was aeons before there were any written documents to furnish us with evidence of early religious ideas and behaviour.

It seems that our distant forefathers were naturally in awe of the powerful forces around them whose manifestations weighed so heavily upon their well-being. Rain, wind, sunshine and darkness, thunder and lightning, stars and rainbows were both fascinating and highly influential in helping or hindering daily activities. Then there was death. What happened when the 'light' went out in somebody's body and their limbs went stiff and cold? Where did their 'soul' go? Did other creatures and objects have such 'spirits'? If so, did these geniuses or demons among other creatures and the forces of nature have power and influence upon humans, and what should be the human response to such powers?

If these were conscious beings like themselves it must be safer to get on good terms with them, to placate them with invocations, offerings and (if necessary) sacrifices. As prayers and propitiatory rites began to be offered to local spirits and gods it must have become appropriate to recognize a hierarchy among them. Durkheim shows how a pre-eminent 'good god' emerges among the lesser deities recognised by Australian tribes. Known by a number of names – but notably as 'Bunjil' – this creator god gathers a whole range of lesser powers under his wing:

> He is called the father of men and they say that he made them … (He).also lighted the sun, heated the earth, made men… animals and trees… gave men the arts of life, arms, language and tribal rites… (Durkheim, (1968, p.287)

He is the general 'benefactor of humanity' – provides for them, responds to them and 'communicates with them, either directly or through intermediaries'. Clearly, Bunjil was regarded by his tribal followers as the Power by which their lives were sustained.

Similarly, as Ninian Smart (1971) points out, on the African continent most cultures recognise a Supreme Power or spirit over-riding the powers of the lesser gods and spirits. In antiquity, among the Greek pantheon Zeus takes the leading role; with the Roman gods Jupiter is supreme. Odin becomes the ruling power among the Norse gods, and Woden (commemorated in our Wednesday) takes pride of place among the Anglo-Saxon gods. It seems, generally, that in these cases polytheism tends to evolve gradually towards a monotheistic situation where one power is regarded as the supreme creator and guardian of mankind; but scholars are divided as to whether this order is necessarily true (see Schmidt F W [1912] *The Origin of the Idea of God)*.

The X Factor in India

For Hindus the vast range of different gods facilitates the invocation of appropriate powers to serve specific callings or meet particular needs, rather like the various saints of Christendom – St Joseph (patron saint of carpenters), St Cecilia (of musicians), St Christopher (of travellers), and St

Jude (of lost causes), etc. But the multitude of gods can also be seen as a spectrum of attitudes and pathways towards the Infinite. The trio of Brahma (the creator), Visnu (the preserver) and Siva (the destroyer), however, are the three most important Hindu gods – controlling the cycle of birth, life and death. Kali (the Mother) is a female deity especially inspiring the devotion of the masses. There is also a ubiquitous godhead *Shakti*, sometimes known in Hinduism as 'The Great Divine Mother' who specifically embodies the active feminine energy of the cosmos and is responsible for both creation and change in the universe.

The complex pluralism and gradual evolution of Hinduism make it hard to pin down the constant themes it comprises, but the idea of an all-embracing Divine, in which humanity shares a part, is fairly constant. The concept of the reincarnation of the individual soul, an important element in the past, may be diminishing now (under the pressure of scientific modernism). The caste system is slowly yielding to the pressure of democracy along with other social reforms in tune with a general humane movement in Western philosophy that runs counter to a fatalistic resignation to whatever a Divine purpose may be believed to be.

Among the ancient texts of Hinduism, *The Upanishads* show 'Brahman' as the holy power animating the whole of reality, sometimes as a personal Lord, sometimes as beyond the reach of our understanding, but clearly the source of our being and preservation. In Part 6 of *The Upanishads* (Mascaro, 1965) it is

> ... by the glory of God that the Wheel of Brahman revolves in the universe...
>
> He is pure consciousness, the creator of time: all-powerful, all knowing. It is under his rule that the work of

creation revolves in its evolution… (p.94)

This view of God or *Brahman* as the power we live by is seen also in the sacred Hindu text, *The Bhagavad-Gita* II, (Mascaro):

'Nowhere I see a beginning or middle or end of thee, O God of all… Thou art…the support of this vast universe… I see thine eyes as the sun and the moon. And I see thy face as a sacred fire that gives light and life to the whole universe in the splendour of a vast offering.' (pp.90-91)

Perhaps, under the influence of Ramakrishna, Vivekananda, Gandhi and others, modern Indian spirituality is moving towards a universalistic recognition of the divine as a power shared by all humanity and approachable by different routes.

Three other faiths arising out of the Hindu complex must be mentioned: Buddhism, Jainism and Sikhism. Buddhism is essentially a 'faith without a god'. As more of a philosophy than a religion it does not come strictly within the terms of a book about God. However, as an important worldwide source of spirituality and ethical values Buddhism can scarcely be ignored. And as a figure, sanctified by time with temples, statues and prayers devoted to him by some of his followers, the Buddha has become a kind of divinity.

Jainism, like Buddhism, does not admit a creator, but the Jains associate themselves very closely with the creative process. They do their utmost to avoid hurting or destroying life, even of the humblest creatures. Among their beliefs, their doctrine that 'no one perspective gives you the whole truth' is one that is an essential aspect of the present exercise. Their attachment to 'Ahimsa' – the principle of non-violence – has become known to the western world through the life and teaching of Gandhi.

Lastly, Sikhism, founded by Nanak (1469-1504), its first guru, was meant to reconcile Hinduism and Islam. It was essentially an attempt to find a faith 'which transcended barriers between religions'. It affirmed that 'there is but one God whose name is true, the Creator, devoid of fear and enmity, immortal, unborn (and) self-existent'. Like the 'God of the X Factor', Guru Nanak's God is both a 'creator' (a Power we live by) and yet a 'mystery'. He declared: 'By thinking I cannot obtain a conception of Him, even though I think hundreds of thousands of times.'

The X Factor in Judaism and Christianity

Turning to Judaism, the first of the three dominant monotheistic religions, God is a name 'not to be uttered'. His essence is beyond human understanding. His chosen people are the Jews and his laws for them are the Ten Commandments entrusted to Moses. These laws (known as the *Decalogue*) – probably derived in part from the earlier *Code of Hammurabi* – make wise provision for the stability of society.

The God of Judaism is said to be a 'jealous' God, demanding the total allegiance of his chosen people who must not make or worship 'graven images' or use his name lightly. In return for their loyalty he promises to look after their welfare. In the book of Genesis (1:28-29) God tells the Hebrews to

> Be fruitful and increase. Fill the earth and subdue it, rule over the fish in the sea, the birds of heaven, and every living thing that moves upon the earth. I will give you all plants that bear seed everywhere on earth, and every tree bearing fruit which yields seed; they shall be yours for food.'

Likewise, in Psalm 24 the poet tells us that the Hebrew God is Creator and Preserver of the world:

> The earth is the Lord's, and the fullness thereof;
> The world, and they that dwell therein.
> For he hath founded it upon the seas,
> And established it upon the floods.

He is concerned, nevertheless, with the protection and well being of the individual, as the psalmist proclaims in Psalm 23:

> The Lord is my shepherd; I shall not want.
> He maketh me to lie down in green pastures;
> He leadeth me beside the still waters.
> He restoreth my soul...

The God of Judaism – the God of the Torah, the Prophets and the Psalms – may be inscrutable, demanding meticulous attention to the details of daily life and fierce in issues of justice, but he remains the source and preserver of life – the power we live by.

The God of traditional Western Christianity is summed up in the Apostles' Creed recited in the formal services of both Protestant and Roman Catholic churches.

> I believe in God the Father Almighty, Maker of heaven and earth; and in Jesus Christ his only Son our Lord, Who was conceived by the Holy Ghost, Born of the Virgin Mary, Suffered under Pontius Pilate, Was crucified, dead, and buried. He descended into hell; The third day he rose again from the dead. He ascended into heaven, and sitteth on the

right hand of God the Father Almighty; from thence he shall come to judge the quick and the dead.

I believe in the Holy Ghost; the holy Catholick Church The Communion of Saints; The Forgiveness of sins; The resurrection of the body; And the life everlasting.

Various denominations and numerous individual Christians will disagree with, or demur from, one or more of these elements. Unitarians, for example, reject the three-person-in-one principle. Some individuals and sects reject the Virgin Birth, others reject the physical Resurrection and so on. Some will think of heaven and hell as places, others as states of mind. Some will demur at the idea of a Day of Judgement and see judgement and forgiveness as part of the daily process of living and acting.

In his recent book *Tokens of Trust* (2010), Rowan Williams examines the meaning of the two principal Christian Creeds explaining their implications and relevance today. As a Quaker, I naturally fight shy of creeds, but I found Dr Williams' interpretation helpful and illuminating. Clearly, whatever differences exist in the wide range of Christian thought, there is no doubt that, for most Christians God is the 'almighty Father' and 'Maker of heaven and earth' – a Power beyond and within us and worthy of worship. As Paul expressed the Christian's duty in the epistle to the Romans:

Let every soul be in subjection to the higher power: for there is no power but from God, and the powers that be are ordained by God.' (Romans 13:1)

The X Factor in Islam
Islam, like Judaism, rejects the idea of a 'Three-Person-in-One' God, though there are many 'names' used to indicate

the qualities of Allah. Of the ninety-nine names found in *The Qur'an*, the two pre-eminent ones, are *Ar-Rahman* (the Beneficent) and *Ar-Rahim* (the Merciful). Other names include: the Peace, the Creator, the Judge, the Patient, the Generous, the Perfect, the Light and the Guide.

In particular, the name of 'Creator' is significant when looking for a common factor between the principle world faiths. Among the many references to Allah's creative powers in *The Quran* we find, (in the *surah* called *The Bee)*:

It is Allah who sends down water from the sky, which provides drink for you, sustains the crops for your cattle's pasture and nourishes the corn and olives, dates and grapes and other fruit... He has directed the day and night, and the sun and moon, into your service; and the stars also serve you by His commandment... On the earth He has created for you all manner of colourful things...It is He who has subjected to you the ocean, so that you may eat of its fresh fish...

A succinct summary of the Muslim attitude to God as Creator can be found in B. Aisha Lemu's *A Student's Guide to Islam* (Macmillan Ed. Ltd, 1976):

We believe that everything is created by a power greater than we ever imagine... He is the One who created everything – the stars, the sun and the moon, the planets, this earth and all the plants and creatures that live on it. He is the One who created you and me. It is by God's power that we live and eat, that we sleep and talk, and study in order to be able to understand more. He is also the One who will take our lives when we die and to Him we shall be returned.

Again, in *Concept of God in Islam,* a recent publication

of the Islamic Propagation Centre International, God is defined as 'The Maker and Sustainer of the world, the Creator of and Provider for man...the 'Active Force and Effective Power in nature'.

X as the Power We Live By

Clearly, In Islam as well as Christianity, Judaism and Hinduism, 'God' (whatever else he or it may be) is 'the Power we Live By'. The same can be said, for example, of Zoroastrianism, where the sun, fire and light feature symbolically as the essential essence of that Power. Even in Buddhism – which does not expressly proclaim a 'god' – we find yoga and *dhyana* among the means of making inward contact with a power that we all live by. And so on, through the wide range of beliefs from animism to New Age thinking. Even atheists recognize a Life-force which can be studied and exploited for human benefit, though not coerced. Thus, a *power* beyond our command, but giving and sustaining our life on this planet, seems to be a constant underlying element in all religions and belief systems.

I hope this brief sampling from some of the major religions sufficiently indicates that despite all their differences there is at least one shared element recognised by the main faiths and even in some ways acknowledged by those of no faith. It is time to explore more closely what this power may be.

CHAPTER THREE

The X Factor as Power

Tyger! Tyger! Burning bright
In the forests of the night,
What immortal hand or eye
Could frame thy fearful symmetry?
William Blake, The Tyger,1794

It is time now to realize the nature of the
universe to which you belong, and of that controlling
Power whose offspring you are; and to understand
that your time has a limit to it. Use it, then, to advance
your enlightenment; or it will be gone, and never
in your power again.
Marcus Aurelius, Meditations c. A.D.179

Our monistic God, the all-embracing essence
of the world, the nature-god of Spinoza and Goethe,
is identical with eternal, all-inspiring energy...
Ernst Haeckel, Der Kampf um den
Entwickelungsgedanken, 1905

A Power Shared by All Creatures

It is clear that, whatever else the major religions believe in, they all recognize God – Zeus, Brahma, Yahweh, Allah, etc – as the *Power by which we live*. It is now time to look more closely at the nature of that power. How can we understand it and how can we relate to it? In what way is the concept of a divinity meaningful to us in the vastness of the twenty-first century cosmos? And what term should we call it?

We all know that we are not responsible for the fact of our own existence. With a little help from our parents we are brought into being by a Power urging life-forms out of the material of our planet. Whether we call this the Source, the Life Force, the First Cause or God, or whether we say it is transcendent, immanent, supernatural or natural, makes little difference to the fact that this Power produces us, gives us a spell of consciousness in the world, and then re-absorbs and recycles the elements of which we are composed. My primary definition of God, then, is *the Power we live by*. But we shall need to look beyond this.

Theologians of diverse faiths have argued variously that this Power is omnipresent, omnipotent, omniscient and omni-benevolent. This is where problems arise. If the power that governs us is *'everywhere, all-powerful and all-knowing'* how can we say that it is also *'all-loving'* when we see so much suffering in the world? To break through this impasse we have to recognise, first, that this power favours a*ll* life (as well as late-comers like ourselves) and, second, that we can know much less about it than many theologians would like us to think.

What we *can* say is that we humans are favoured beyond other creatures by our capacity to explore and understand the world intellectually, imaginatively and creatively. Blessed with language, our power to conceptualise and communicate gives us considerable advantages over all other creatures in terms of appreciating, controlling or adapting to and (arguably) enjoying the world we inhabit. However, our language and all our knowledge and power remain *inherent* in the Creative Power – they *derive* from this source since there is no other.

Attempts to Define Deity

Over past centuries deep-thinking individuals – philosophers, theologians, poets, prophets and sages – have tried in different ways to define the power we live by. In Hebrew literature He (or It) is described in turn as a *provider, a guide and leader, mighty and terrible, glorious, our refuge and strength, a judge* and *a king*, etc. Moses, however, is said to have received from God the simple but enigmatic message: *I am that I am.* The Christian *New Testament* confirms some of the foregoing definitions and also includes *(a being) to be feared, a consuming fire, a non-respecter of persons, Alpha and Omega (the beginning and the end), a spirit* and *love*. When St Paul declares to the Athenians that he can now reveal 'the unknown God' to them he is, of course, referring to Jesus.

From a more secular angle, the Roman emperor Marcus Aurelius offers in his *Meditations* a whole range of conceptions of this power. It is the *primal Cause* 'like a river in flood bearing everything along', *the divine Cause*, the *World-Mind* 'willing each separate happening', *the Whole, the Creative Reason of the universe,* the controlling *Power* whose offspring we are, *Truth, Nature* 'the original creator of all true things', *God* and sometimes *the Gods*. Some would regard this diversity of expressions as muddled thinking, an unhealthy mish-mash of conceptions. But his all-embracing attitude can also be seen as an example of 'joined-up thinking' – bringing together many aspects of one central concept. The following passage from his *Meditations* bears witness to his holistic outlook:

> All things are interwoven with one another; a sacred bond unites them; there is scarcely one thing that is isolated from another. Everything is coordinated, everything works together in giving form to the one universe. The world-order is a unity made up of multiplicity: God is one, pervading all things; all being is one, all law is one (namely the common reason which all thinking creatures possess) and all truth is one...

I have characterized Marcus Aurelius as 'secular' only in the sense that he is not committed to a particular religious line. He is open-minded, but he is undoubtedly 'spiritual' as the following quotation demonstrates:

> To those who insist, 'where have you ever seen the gods, and how can you be so assured of their existence, that you worship them in this way?' my answer is, 'For one thing, they are perfectly visible to the eye [as stars]. For another, I have never seen my own soul either, but none the less do I venerate that. So it is with the gods; it is experience which proves their power every day, and therefore I am satisfied that they exist and I do them reverence.

Marcus Aurelius' reference to the stars as gods is intriguing: did he think of the planets Mars, Jupiter, Venus, etc, as shining divinities, or as symbols of the divine? There are no clues to this mystery in his *Meditations* as far as I can see. However, his spiritual conception of the 'soul' is easier to understand.

For Islam, six centuries later, the power we live by is *The Light of the Heavens and the Earth* and *our Creator.*

But the same power is also given a number of attributes stressing anthropomorphic titles and qualities: *our Lord, our King, the Beneficent, the Merciful and the Forgiving* among others. Allah seems to be almost as much a person as a power.

Baruch Spinoza, in the 17th century, generally prefers theological abstractions, defining God as *'a being absolutely infinite; a substance consisting of infinite attributes, each of which expresses His eternal and infinite essence.'* But he hits the mark admirably with: *'the power by which we preserve our being.'*

A century later, in *An Essay on Man*, the poet Alexander Pope moves from the abstract *'universal Cause'* and *'the great directing mind of all'* to echoes of Marcus Aurelius, for example in the lines:

All are but parts of one stupendous whole,
Whose body Nature is, and God the soul...

In the same poem, the good person for Pope is a 'slave to no sect' who *'looks through nature up to nature's God.'* Surprisingly perhaps for an eighteenth-century poet, Pope prefigures the coming Romantic époque in declaring that 'The state of nature was the reign of God'.

This raises the question put to me by a colleague: 'Isn't the X Factor God "The Power we live by" simply another way of saying Mother Nature?' The answer is to some extent contained in Alexander Pope's couplet just quoted. When we think of Mother Nature we tend to visualize the embodiments of nature – mountains and valleys, lakes and streams, animals and birds. And we frequently see them in a romanticized manner. The term Mother Nature tends to conjure up the product rather than the process. But when I use the expression 'the Power we live by' my concern is essentially with the process – the power behind nature, the 'soul' of the universe, the energy and spirit that animates it.

Definitions in the Age of Science

In the late 19th Century, Matthew Arnold deplored the attempts of theologians to give quasi-scientific definitions of God. He preferred looser, but suggestive, expressions such as 'the stream of tendency by which all things seek to fulfil the law of their being' or 'the eternal *not ourselves* that makes for righteousness'.

The effect of a series of works such as Darwin's *Origin of Species,* Arnold's *Literature and Dogma,* Thomas Huxley's scientific and Freud's psychological writings, was to prepare the twentieth century for new approaches to defining the power we live by. William James, for example, in *The Varieties of Religious Experience (1902)* writes:

> The God whom science recognises must be a God of universal laws exclusively...He cannot accommodate his processes to the convenience of individuals.

And Julian Huxley (the grandson of Thomas Huxley) writes in *Essays of a Biologist*:

> The change in our conception of God necessitates the stressing of religious experience as such, as against belief in particular dogma, or in the efficacy of special ritual.

And even William Temple, when Archbishop of Canterbury, offered the intriguing observation (for a man of the cloth) that *'It is a mistake to suppose that God is only, or even chiefly, concerned with religion.'* In other words, the Creative Power has wider concerns than his devotees can conceptualise.

Mohandas Gandhi, whose spirituality was famously more intense than most of his contemporaries of whatever persuasion, went further than the Archbishop in proposing that *'God has no religion'*. Rather like Marcus Aurelius, the Mahatma characterizes the power we live by in terms of a range of concepts, seen for example in the following passage from *Harijan (March 1940)*:

> I do not regard God as a person. Truth for me is God, and God's laws are not different things or facts, in the sense that an earthly king and his law are different. Because God is an Idea, Law Himself... He and His Law abide everywhere and govern everything. Therefore, I do not think that He answers in every detail every request of ours, but there is no doubt that He rules our action and I literally believe that not a blade of grass grows or moves without His will.

Here God is *Truth, Law, an Idea, ubiquitous, impersonal* and yet very much in control.

So far, I have only quoted those sources who are unfazed by the term 'God' when discussing the power we live by. Among those in the twentieth century who find the term embarrassing are Christopher Hitchens (*God is Not Great, USA, 2007*) and Richard Dawkins (*The God Delusion, UK, 2006*). Like many of us, Dawkins is deeply disturbed by the evils and injustices committed in the name of religion in the past and by the problems brought about by violent clashes between rival faiths in the global society we now inhabit. He believes that advances in scientific knowledge, and particularly developments in our under-standing of evolution since the publication of *The Origin of Species,* make religion both irrelevant and a positive danger in today's world. To fill the 'God-shaped gap' after the abandonment of religious faith he recommends 'a good dose of science, the honest and systematic endeavour to find out the truth about the real world'.

Dawkins rightly says: 'each of us builds, inside our head, a model of the world in which we find ourselves'. I heartily agree with this, but whereas Dawkins would like our models to exclude any concept of 'God', I believe it is time for the adherents and leaders of the major faiths to be revising their internalized models in keeping with the demands of the twenty-first century *Zeitgeist*, if humanity and civilization are to survive. I share with Dawkins a respect amounting almost to reverence for the great achievement of Charles Darwin in revolutionizing our understanding of human evolution in the natural world, and a deep respect for scientific method and scientific progress in general. But I cannot agree that we can easily dispense with the term 'God', nor with religion in one form or another. I would recommend (along with 'a good dose of science') a good dose of semantics, so that people better understand the use and meaning of religious terms and scriptures.

I want here to question some of Dawkins' observations that I find misguided. First his avowal:

> I am not attacking any particular version of God or gods. I am attacking God, all gods, anything and everything supernatural, wherever and whenever they have been or will be invented. (p. 36)

This seems to be a blunderbuss of a statement. (If all the targets from such a volley were to be hit a great deal of good would be destroyed.) In the first place, there is nothing supernatural in 'the power we live by' which as we have seen is the vital shared element of godhead in all the major religions. This power is essentially *natural*, although because it can command our respect, reverence and awe, it evokes in many thoughtful people a spiritual response. Apparently what Dawkins is really intending to attack is not so much 'God' as *Religion at large*, since religions – unlike 'the power we live by' – are admittedly 'invented' by mankind, otherwise they would not be so varied and contentious. Secondly, if Dawkins is attacking superstition and miracles contrary to nature many devout people would agree with him. Not everyone in church, synagogue or mosque is still living in the thought-world of the middle ages. For many religious people nowadays the *miracle of creation* itself is quite enough to engage our reverence without the need for miraculous demonstrations.

By 'creation', of course, I am not referring to 'Creation*ism*', a modern misinterpretation of ancient poetry, but to the wonders of the universe in which we find ourselves. On this issue, Dawkins quotes Carl Sagan (*Pale Blue Dot, 1995)* in support of his attack on God:

> A religion, old or new, that stressed the magnificence of the Universe as revealed by modern science might be able to draw forth reserves of reverence and awe hardly tapped by the conventional faiths.

There is a lot in this, but why only *'as revealed by modern science'?* True, we are now learning more and more about the extraordinary mysteries of nature both at the cosmic and micro levels, but were religious people unaware of the magnificence of our environment before the recent scientific discoveries? Surely, throughout the centuries, both scriptural and secular poets have offered eloquent evidence to the contrary. In any case science only *reveals and employs* these awesome aspects of our world – science is not the Power itself. Dawkins Quotes Carl Sagan again:

> ...if by "God" one means the set of physical laws that govern the universe, then clearly there is such a God. This God is emotionally unsatisfying...it does not make much sense to pray to the law of gravity.

This observation begs a lot of questions. For one thing 'the law of gravity', although an extremely important concept, is not an adequate description of 'the physical laws that govern the universe' in their totality, and neither the one nor the other expression has the full meaning or resonance of 'the power we live by'. Whatever our understanding of these concepts, most people would prefer to use a term like 'God' (or one of its translations) for the purposes of prayer or worship.

Quoting Steven Weinberg (*Dreams of a Final Theory*), Dawkins objects to the fact that 'some people have views of God that are so broad and flexible that they will find God wherever they look for him even "in a lump of coal".' So what? It is equally true that we can find God 'in a nutshell'. The idea that God is ubiquitous is certainly not a new one, and when a lump of coal is aflame it is in some way responding to that same Power *we* live by – perhaps reminding us that we are all made of stardust if we look back far enough. Similarly, God 'in a nutshell' reminds us that the hidden kernel is carrying the sacred seed of life from time immemorial into the future; it is both fact and symbol of the eternal energy of creation. From Marcus Aurelius to Mohandas Gandhi a great number of thinkers have used the term God in 'a broad and flexible way' without detriment to their powers of thought or of beneficent action.

Dawkins refers to 'the pantheistic reverence which many of us share with its most distinguished exponent,

Albert Einstein', and complains that 'much unfortunate confusion is caused by failure to distinguish what can be called Einsteinian religion from supernatural religion.' There is some justice in this. My own faith is certainly closer to Einstein's pantheistic religion than to 'supernatural religion'. However, Einstein does not reject the term 'God' with the same vehemence as Dawkins; he used it rather in the sense that Gandhi used it, representing 'law' or 'truth' or 'the nature of things'. For example, in expressing his objections to the quantum theory, he declared 'God is subtle, but he is not malicious' and 'God does not play dice with the cosmos'. More significantly, as late as 1940, when he was turned 60, he apparently believed that 'science without religion is lame, [and] religion without science is blind'. I think this distinguishes Einstein's attitude from that of Dawkins, who is in danger of making either the intellect, or science, or perhaps Charles Darwin, into a god.

Einstein, in fact, apparently stated that 'we should take care not to make the intellect our god: it has, of course, powerful muscles, but no personality.' [In *Barnes and Noble Book of Quotations*, ed. Robert I. Fitzhenry, 'Intellect'] It is interesting that Einstein used the term 'personality' to describe what he felt *intellect* lacked when it comes to an object worthy of reverence. But discussion of the concept of 'personality' in relation to deity must be postponed until chapter 7, which will deal with anthropomorphism.

The Problem of Divine 'Purpose'
However, it may be useful here to discuss one problem relating to anthropomorphism which frequently arises in consideration of the nature of the Power we live by: the question of 'God's purpose'. For example, a Benedictine

monk recently pronounced on the radio: *'There is a purpose in life and God is in control'*. This seems to me an extraordinary assertion. It amounts virtually to an insult to the divinity. If both propositions were true it would be high time to change the controller. What kind of god would organize the mayhem daily recorded in our media. Thomas Hobbes was at least partly right in declaring that (for too many) 'the life of man is solitary, poor, nasty, brutish and short'. The very term 'Act of God' nowadays normally means a disaster, and to such natural disasters we must add the acts of mankind including war and torture, 'ethnic cleansing', domestic violence, 'crusades', factory farming and... how many more impediments to human and animal well-being? A 'controlling' god whose *purpose* was the situation we witness daily on the media would scarcely be worthy of reverence.

Problems arise when discussing 'divine purpose' because of our anthropomorphic tendencies. Just because *we* have what we call 'purposes' it is assumed that the creative power operates in the same way. But we have no evidence to assume this. Everything, living and inanimate, in the world is a manifestation of some aspect of the power we live by – but it is *we* who experience or invent purposes – to find food and shelter, or a mate, for example: or (when basic needs are satisfied) to compose music, make models, or collect stamps, or (for the more ambitious) to build cities and empires. In speaking of the power we live by it is more appropriate to think not in terms of purpose, but of urge, impulse or dynamic. God – the power we live by – *enables* us to pursue our purposes, but in their pursuit we are responsible for such forms of control as can be imposed on our efforts, individually and collectively. God provides the stage, the actors and the props, but he doesn't write the scripts, nor direct the play. God is the producer; man the director. And whether the result is a comedy or a tragedy is largely our responsibility.

Freewill and predetermination

The question of our responsibility for the exercise of the power at our disposal brings us to the vexed issue of freewill and determinism. Are we responsible for our actions, or are they preordained? Since all events are determined by preexistent causes, the doctrine that 'individual human beings have no free will and cannot be held morally responsible for their actions' is very persuasive. Marcus Aurelius was apparently persuaded by it. 'Has any good fortune befallen thee?' he asks himself, and answers: 'If so, it has been predestined since the beginning of the world.' The Christian church was divided about it, but both Luther and Calvin believed it. According to Calvin:

'Predestination we call the eternal decree of God, whereby He has determined what...would have to become of every individual of mankind. Eternal life is ordained for some, and eternal damnation for others, (*Institutes of the Christian Religion III, 1536*).

A century later, the philosopher Descartes declared equally presumptuously: 'That God has foreordained everything is self-evident.'

Of course, nothing happens by pure chance: there are always causes of natural events and – in the human sphere – there are causes limiting the choices we can make and influencing the actions and events that follow. But that doesn't mean that everything is planned – that the Power we live by has got it all mapped out. The fact is that although every human decision is circumscribed by preliminary facts (causes), the decision itself can be freely made within those limitations. The result of this (of course, relatively) free decision will inevitably create a new field of existent facts and causes within which future decisions, by all those concerned, can be freely made. This is one of the reasons why it is impossible to predict the future with absolute certainty. We can foresee tendencies, but the ground is continually shifting, owing to the freely taken decisions made by individuals and communities. The 2009 Credit Crunch and the so-called Arab Spring of 2011 are cases in point!

Dawkins cites Phillip E Johnson in suggesting that 'Darwinism is the story of humanity's liberation from the delusion that its destiny is controlled by a power higher than itself.' There is some truth in this, since the theory of natural selection reveals clearly the processes of how things *evolve* gradually in the natural world; there are clearly causes and effects, but no evidence of a divine (or any other) overall advance Planning. And in the world of ideas, the same principles hold true – ideas *evolve* from one to another, gradually and continually changing the field of discourse and creating the cultural *Zeitgeist* for each generation.

Nature evolves, culture evolves and religions evolve. God, understood as 'the Power we live by', does not evolve as far as we know; it is doubtless the same power for all time and everywhere, but its *manifestations* evolve. Our earth has changed its form since it was flung as a mass from its mother, the sun; the creatures inhabiting it have evolved from primeval slime, through unthinking swimming, flying and land-moving giants to a wonderful range of creatures including human beings and domesticated animals. Human beings would appear to be the first creatures able to ask questions about their origins and reasons for existing. 'Who, or what put us here?' we want to know, and 'are we the responsibility of, or responsible to, a benevolent power concerned with our welfare?'

Morality and the power we live by

This last question surfaces particularly at times of natural catastrophes. When tsunamis, earthquakes and volcanoes strike, or when they are visited by plagues and other afflictions, humans ask a question no other creature has ever asked before: is this power we live by *good*? In an attempt to answer this, we have to take a broad sweep. The problem arises because the power *we* live by is also the power enjoyed by every other living creature whether friendly or hostile to us.

The author of Genesis was indulging in wishful thinking when he proposed that God gave man dominion 'over every living thing that moveth upon earth.' True, we have gone a long way in this direction, but there is no evidence to suggest that the creative Power is any less concerned with other life forms than with ourselves. In sheer numbers humans are overwhelmed both by the range of species created and the astonishing fecundity of some of these species. Some of our least favourite – ants, for instance – do very well! So much for divine favouritism – at least when it comes to numbers.

The power we live by is universally friendly to its productions: it is the primal urge to create, sustain and protect its creatures. The downside of this is seen in the food chain: most creatures have to provide meals for the next one up on the list! Their Creator has, however, given each of them the best means of protecting themselves that circumstances could devise; consequently many species (as distinct from individuals) have shown a remarkable capacity to survive. Tennyson, in a pessimistic mood, saw the situation as 'Nature red in tooth and claw'; but despite the natural wastage the system involves, the very fecundity of the Creative Power means an extraordinary number and variety of living creatures at least get a look in, and many of us are very glad of it, despite having to cope with our fair share of 'the ills that flesh is heir to'. Many people are so attached to their life that they want it to go on for ever. Others of us are happy to inhabit the eternal life-stream for a brief spell, fully aware that it can continue quite satisfactorily without us after our demise, but also knowing that we will have contributed our halfpennyworth for good or ill to the ongoing story.

At least we are not the puppets of a controller. We may even be the chief means of performing the work or 'will' of the Power we live by since that same power is both immanent and transcendent. In the aftermath of the 2005 tsunami some writers found 'God in the hands of those who helped'those suffering from the catastrophe; others blamed 'God' for allowing such incidents; yet others saw the *tsunami* as a punishment for sin. These last two reactions occur in the minds of those whose conception of 'God' is stretched beyond 'the Power we live by'. It seems to me quite unfair to conceive a god in too broad terms and then to blame 'him' or 'it' for not coming up to expectations. Although tsunamis, earthquakes and volcanoes ultimately derive from the same natural power that gives us life, they should not be seen as hostile forces; they are the inevitable result of physical pressures that build up and must find release. As to 'punishment', the power we live by has no such concerns. It fosters life without judgement. In an article in *The Guardian,* Martin Kettle points out:

> The [2005] tsunami generated by the quake made no attempt to differentiate between the religions of those whom it made its victims. Hindus were swept away in India, Muslims were carried off in Indonesia, Buddhists in Thailand, (and) visiting Christians and Jews received no special treatment either.

He adds that for the scientific belief system, 'this poses no problem. Here, it says, was a mindless natural event.' Of course, we should do what we can to learn from such events and find ways of reducing their disastrous consequences, just as (as some writers pointed out) we should find ways of learning from the horrific consequences of man-made disasters. (The Iraqi war – they pointed out – was going on at the same time.)

The question as to whether 'God'the power we live by is 'good' is primarily a semantic question – what do we mean by 'good'? – and so will be visited again in chapter 8 dealing with moral issues. However, as Dawkins reminds us from a scientific viewpoint, 'we live not only on a friendly planet but also in a friendly universe'. Such 'friendliness', at least, seems to represent goodness on the part of the power we live by. This is apparently the 'Anthropic principle' which 'states that, since we are alive, eucaryotic and conscious, our planet has to be one of the intensely rare planets that has bridged all three gaps.'

To this reassurance we can add that on this friendly planet humanity has made considerable progress in discovering the power of love and principles of justice. These discoveries come from within ourselves and from those around us. They must, at least partially, be expressions of the power we live by, and the mental activity by which the discoveries are made derives from this power. We have good cause, then, to adopt an attitude of respect, or reverence, for life. We are fortunate to have some of our number – poets, prophets, scientists, novelists and philosophers – who can help us on our way.

We are indeed lucky to be alive – at any rate, you and I are – able and free to read and write. Evolution and the power we live by have brought us to this point. Along with all living creatures, however, we are powered by the same ultimate source. In our case, as mammalian humans, once the umbilical cord is cut, and we leave dependence within our mother's womb, we remain harnessed to a sort of 'remote dynamo' by which we are daily recharged. The power is not our own – but given, or loaned, while we have breath. People take medicines, have operations, do exercises, and go to no end of trouble, in order to hang on to that power as long as possible! Apparently we think life is 'a good thing'.

It is perhaps helpful to see the power we live by as operating at four different levels – physical, vegetal, animal and spiritual. (1) The basic physical level is being steadily revealed by scientific research: the dynamic, sub-atomic electromagnetic level – the realm of photons, electrons, protons, neutrons, quarks and molecules that inhabit *all* matter. The hills are (almost literally) alive with a vibrant energy of their own. The fragment of quartz in our modern watches offers a constant reminder of this.

(2) Next, at the vegetal level, with the advent of life-informing DNA, the same power creates the vegetable world of essentially immobile life forms, non-sentient – but striving, adapting and steadily changing to fulfil their destiny. (3) Then comes animal life in all its complexity, mobile and inquisitive, leading to humans capable of linguistic communication, introspection and conceptualization. (4) Finally, there is the spiritual level. But that is more appropriately considered in the next chapter dealing with 'God' or 'X' as mystery.

CHAPTER FOUR

X as Mystery

> *God moves in a mysterious way.*
> *His wonders to perform.*
> William Cowper,
> Light Shining out of the Darkness, 1779

> *The most beautiful thing we*
> *can experience is the mysterious. It is the*
> *source of all true art and science.*
> Albert Einstein, What I Believe, 1934

> *We used to think that science*
> *would answer all our questions and*
> *solve all our mysteries, but the*
> *more we learn, the more mysterious*
> *our world becomes.*
> Karen Armstrong,
> The Spiral Staircase, 2004

The enigmatic X

When in 1799 Napoleon asked the Comte de Laplace what room there was for God in the cosmology of his five-volume work *Celestial Mechanics*, Laplace replied: 'Sire, I had no room for that hypothesis.' Now, in the twenty-first century, there is even more space in the cosmos, yet many of today's physicists would still be hard put to find room for God in it. They have enough on their hands with an expanding universe, Big Bangs, black holes and now (at the other extreme) the subatomic Higgs boson.

Our particular galaxy is now known to be composed of some 100 billion stars. Its halo is about 50 thousand light-years across and there is possibly a massive black hole – a kind of solar vacuum cleaner – at its centre. Fortunately our sun is about two thirds of the way out from the centre and (for the time being anyway) out of danger! Thanks to the telescopes of William Herschel, a contemporary of Laplace, we learnt that our sun is only one of a multitude of stars in the Milky Way. And we now know that there are billions of galaxies in the universe, some of them bigger than our own. Not only is our universe some ten billion light-years in diameter, but we are now informed that it is quite probably only part of a 'multiverse'.

All this is 'light-years' away from the second century conception of the cosmos in Ptolemy's *Almagest*, which was the recognised explanation right up to the discoveries of Copernicus and Galileo in the late Renaissance. When most of the scriptures of our religions today were written it was generally believed that our world was the centre of the universe, man was the pinnacle of creation and God, or a whole pantheon of gods, was keeping watch on us from heaven above.

By the time Laplace 'had no room' for the hypothesis of a divine Creator there were already serious doubts among scientists and philosophers on the subject. Voltaire, for example, seems to have been ambivalent about God's existence. In a letter to Frederick the Great he wrote: 'My reason tells me that God exists, but it also tells me that I can never know what he is' (Oct, 1737).

But Voltaire was by no means the first to be perplexed about the nature of God. In the *Old Testament* story of the 'Burning bush' (*Exodus 3.2-14*) Moses is said to have asked God: 'If I go to the Israelites and tell them that the God of their forefathers has sent me to them, and they ask me his name, what shall I say?'

And God is said to have answered enigmatically: 'I AM; that is who I am. Tell them that I AM has sent you to them.'

Apparently Moses was still perplexed, because God is said to have added: 'Tell the Israelites... that it is JEHOVAH, the God of their forefathers...'

Moses was evidently still disconcerted, and was only too glad to put the delivery of the message into the hands of his brother, Aaron, the Levite.

In the *New Testament*, the Evangelist *John,* begins his Gospel with something of a conundrum, declaring: 'In the beginning was the Word, and the Word was with God, and the Word was God.' (1:1-2) Scholars still debate the precise meaning of this. The Greek words 'Logos' (related to 'lego' meaning 'speak') signifies both 'word' and 'meaning'. John seems to be using it in the sense of 'the meaning, or the principle governing the cosmos'. The double meaning of 'Logos' in Greek is useful for John (and for later theologians) because *meaning* is silent and *speech* is vocal sound, so it can stand for God as the (silent) Creator and Jesus as the (vocal) Mediator. When to this is added the 'Spirit' descending at Jesus's baptism' (1:22), all is set for the concept of the Trinity. John was not, of course, proposing this doctrine since he declares a few lines later that, 'No man has seen God at any time' (1:18) and he refers to Jesus simply as the Son explaining and demonstrating his Father's significance. (The doctrine of the Trinity, some two centuries later, may have been useful for Christianity perhaps, but it upset and confused both Jews and, in due course, Mohammed.) It is almost certainly the same John, in his first Epistle, who offers a further definition of the divine power: 'God is love' (4:16) an intangible, but highly evocative concept. This, although essentially a poetic statement, is certainly a good enough principle and attitude to live by.

God can be just as enigmatic and intangible in Islam as in Christianity. Take the description of Allah by a twelfth century Muslim, Abdallah Ibn Tumart, in his 'Confession of Faith':

Time does not contain [Allah], nor space hold Him. No intelligence can grasp Him, nor imagination figure Him. Nothing is like Him. But still He hears and sees all things. *Tauhid* (c.1140)

In all three faiths referred to above, there are so many names, definitions and descriptions of the divinity available – loving, long-suffering, wise, mighty, wrathful, avenging and so on – that according to our inclinations we can virtually take our pick of God's nature and respond accordingly. No doubt we should heed the advice of the sixteenth century Anglican theologian Richard Hooker:

Our soundest knowledge is to know that we know Him not as indeed He is [therefore]...our safest eloquence concerning

Him is our silence, when we confess …that His glory is inexplicable, His greatness above our capacity to reach.
The Laws of Ecclesiastical Polity (1594)

The advice of Goethe, whose nature leaned both towards science and spirituality, is equally useful in such matters:

Let us fathom the things that are fathomable and reserve the unfathomable for reverence and quietude. (quoted in *The Week*, (19.4.2008).

Mystery and the scientific spirit

At the end of the previous chapter I suggested that 'X' – the Power we live by – has four levels: subatomic, vegetal, animal and finally – spiritual. In the last, more abstract and intangible area, we risk running foul of the scientific spirit that likes to be able to weigh and measure material and visible data before it reaches any conclusions. Unfortunately we cannot see or measure 'X'. However, we can admire its manifestations that are all around us, and we can sense and revere its grandeur. Few people go around in a continual glow of divine exaltation, but most of us find that our spirits are raised at certain moments – perhaps by a beautiful sunset, a purring cat, a baby's smile, an exceptional painting or musical performance; and for the more devout through intense meditation or prayer.

It is difficult to know whether other creatures experience any spiritual rapport with their environment. Possibly, since they are not separated from nature as we humans are by the intervention of language, the 'lower' animals may have a richer spiritual relation to their surroundings than we have! Who can say? It is almost certainly true that young children, unencumbered by a weight of linguistic conceptions, and therefore nearer to nature, are more able to capture a sense of the numinous than adults are. Some poets, such as Thomas Traherne, William Wordsworth, and Dylan Thomas seem able to recollect a child's view of the world unfazed by the awe-inspiring mystery of existence. Traherne achieves it for example in *Centuries of Meditation* (1670) and Dylan Thomas in *A Child's Christmas in Wales* (1954). Wordsworth, in *Intimations of Immortality* (*1807*), regretted how a child's spiritual response to the world gradually changes in the process of growing up. 'Heaven lies about us in our infancy!' he wrote, but approaching adulthood 'Shades of the prison-house begin to close / Upon the growing boy'. For a while in his journey the child holds on to life as a splendid vision. But, regrettably: 'At length the man perceives it die away / And fade into the light of common day.'

It does seem true that most adults lose something of the child's capacity to respond directly and rapturously to the world about us. As we wrap our experience around with explanatory language and gain increasing command of our surroundings we lose something of the sense of immediacy, mystery and colour our environment had for us earlier. This is the price we pay for becoming knowledgeable and 'worldly-wise'. The poet Keats expresses his regret at this phenomenon. In his poem *Lamia* (1819) he asks: 'Do not all charms fly / At the mere touch of cold philosophy?' and gives as an example the inevitable change in our conception of a rainbow when we learn the scientific reason for the phenomenon. Some of the impact of its beauty dissolves as it falls into 'the dull catalogue of common things'. This is brought home to some of us today as the once 'wandering moon' of poetry has lost something of its lustre and mystery since men have landed on it and scraped bits of dust from it.

It seems that science and mystery can be uncomfortable bedfellows. Richard Dawkins points out the fact that 'mystics exult in mystery and want it to stay mysterious,' whereas 'Scientists exult in mystery for a different reason: it gives them something to do.' He is certainly right about the scientists. Some neuroscientists, for example, are currently investigating the human brain, searching for what they call a 'god neuron' – dealing with love, creativity and morals. This would presumably equate with the 'spirit' – 'the animating or life-giving principle in a person or animal' or 'the intelligent non-physical part of a person; the soul' (*Oxford English Reference Dictionary*). It will be interesting to know what they do with the 'god neuron' if they find it. Presumably, this will tie up the higher spiritual level of the Power we live by with the basic subatomic level referred to earlier. Whether the neuroscientists can discover this element among the billions of neurons and synapses in the human cortex is another matter. For the time being, 'God' at both the macro and micro level remains shrouded in mystery. This, however, is unlikely to worry the general population judging by a cull of recent statistics suggesting that a steadily increasing number seem to revel in mystery.

How scientifically-minded is the U.K. population today?

At the end of 2009, *The Week (26 December)* assembled some interesting statistical data collected over the year. It seems that:

39% of U.K. citizens believe in ghosts (compared with 10% in 1950);

22% believe in astrology (compared with 7% in 1950) (*Mori/Telegraph poll*);

51% believe evolution isn't enough to explain the complexity of life on Earth;

33% believe that 'God created the world some time in the past 10,000 years'.

(*ComRes/Guardian*).

Among other data related to religion (according to a *Theos/Guardian* Survey):

70% believe in the human soul;

53% in life after death;

44% in the east of England 'say the theory of evolution makes God obsolete'.

However (in a *Mori/Times Survey*):

20% of Londoners have never heard of Charles Darwin!

Judging by these figures, the average man-in-the street is probably a lot less interested in the neuroscientists' discoveries about the 'god neuron' than professional scientists are. However, Dawkins makes a fair point in suggesting that 'one of the truly bad effects of religion is that it teaches us that it is a *virtue* to be satisfied with not understanding.' [My italics] There *is* nothing virtuous in shutting one's mind to new insights that might help us to understand the world we live in.

Personally, I am quite happy to accept the popular concept of the 'soul' – 'God's breath' to some. To Quakers it is the extraordinary 'inner light' that animates our physical being. However, I must confess to being shocked at the statistics quoted above relating to a general ignorance of the time-scale of our world and of the process of evolution within it. I also find the increase in the belief in ghosts and astrology disturbing. I sympathize with those who hope that their soul will continue to live independently after death, but do not personally anticipate this. My view, as a Christian humanist, is that we all *participate* in the eternal process, and leave our mark (for good or ill) for those who follow.

It seems that the doctrine of a future life came to the West largely via Greek and Asiatic thinking under the influence of Orphism. Bertrand Russell points out (in *The History of Western Philosophy, p.350)* that although 'Elements of mystery religions, both Orphic and Asiatic, enter largely into Christian theology' in all of them, 'the central myth is that of the dying god who rises again', rather than a future life for the population at large. However, according to Gibbon (in the *Fall of the Roman Empire)* as the idea of a *divine* resurrection gradually became generalized to include all 'believers'this may have added to the appeal and growth of the early church. Inevitably, the appeal of a future life after death still has its attractions. This may be simply a matter of wishful thinking. In any case it cannot be either proved or disproved. Arguments from 'near-death experiences', etc, have very little weight since they are inevitably recounted by the still living; and the 'evidence' from spiritualists' séances is recognized to be highly unreliable.

Although most people, religious and otherwise, seem to be content with mysteries, not all religious people are mystics. Only a minority, for example, shares the kind of visionary insights of Traherne, Wordsworth and Keats (quoted above). The majority of faithful Christians, Muslims, Jews and others are doubtless too busy with the everyday business of living to devote much time to entering ecstatic trances. On the other hand they probably lack the scientific background or taste for unravelling mysteries. In any case there is no need to be concerned about the mystery of a possible afterlife, or about miracles against nature, if we believe God is 'the Power we live by', since this power is an ever present fact of life. It is Life itself, and although its origin and precise nature remain a mystery, it is the power to which we owe everything, including the power to conceive it.

There are many thoughtful believers who don't 'exult' in mystery but respect it alongside a healthy respect for science. They simply recognise that the kind of evidence science can provide is not appropriate for identifying divinity. The German pastor Dietrich Bonhoeffer (who, incidentally, Dawkins respects) was committed to prison for his Christian faith under the Nazi regime. In his *Letters and Papers from Prison* Bonhoeffer refers in places to 'God as a working hypothesis'. (Unlike the Comte de Laplace, Bonhoeffer *did* have room for the hypothesis.) He accepts that the Power we live by is a 'mystery', suggesting in his book *No Rusty Swords* that 'a God who let us prove his existence would be an idol'. Despite (or because of) his deeply held religious convictions, Bonhoeffer had his feet on the ground, so to speak, since he is chiefly concerned with 'life *before* death' rather than after it. He was an example to his fellow prisoners up to the time of his execution, and their testimony, as well as that of others, reveals a person fully committed to a power beyond ourselves which – although an unproven mystery – was ever present in his life.

X and evolution

Of all our body parts, it's probably our navel that gets the least consideration. But it's well worth 'contemplating our navel' (as some sages recommend) if only for a brief moment. Imagine for a few seconds that the umbilical cord attaching us to our mother had not been cut, and hers to her mother, and so on *ad infinitum.* Not a pretty sight! We would soon be in a tangle. And, of course, it's impossible. Each generation has to be freed from the last. But if we stop to think about it that largely undervalued cord links us to the past like a string of pearls, or better like a lifeline, to antiquity. From mother to mother (with the brief intervention of a father for each generation) the umbilical life-line takes us back through the middle ages and the dark ages, the Roman, Greek and Babylonian imperial eras to the first *homo sapiens* and beyond to the first hominid. Creationists will presumably stop with Eve as their ultimate relative. But most of us will continue well beyond that to when the mothers (and incidental fathers) begin to get smaller and hairier.

At some distant stage the line becomes a sort of 'dotted line' when our female forebears – looking very different – no doubt laid eggs and took rather less care of us. Eventually we finish up – or rather start out – as some kind of protozoa in the primal soup where life began on planet earth. On the way our forebears somehow achieved consciousness and finally self-consciousness and that amazing 'light'somewhere inside our heads that enables us to 'see' images even with our eyes closed. Thanks to that long succession of evolving 'mothers' we become another piece of the world knowing itself. (Why we inherit our fathers' names when our mothers undertake the major role in the process I shall never understand.)

The mysterious 'X' – the Power we live by – is, of course, the driving power behind the evolutionary process, and Darwin's theory, consistently supported by accumulating evidence from a range of scientific disciplines, is the only reasonable way we have today of making sense of our geological and biological history. But it has to be remembered that the evolution theory is not itself the *Power of creation*; it is a brilliant *description* of the way this power operates – the *how*. The Power itself remains a mystery and people are still fascinated by the *Why*? Why is the Power there? Why are we its beneficiaries? (Or for the less fortunate among us: why do they have to suffer existence at this Power's behest?)

Nevertheless, our questions such as 'How did it get there?' and 'Who or what started it?' lead us nowhere but into infinite regression. Even theories such as the Big Bang result in further causal questions. Pursuing infinity and eternity in search of their limits is apparently a fruitless exercise: and the search for the reason and origin of the creation of our cosmos, cradled miraculously in space and time, ends ultimately with a question mark. All the wonderful scientific advances in physics, genetics, nanotechnology and astronomy are discoveries and descriptions, not ultimate reasons, and are certainly not the Power itself. In its genetic engineering experiments, for example, biotechnology must follow the rules of that Power. We must not confuse science with the Power itself. This, I think, Dawkins and a number of other atheists are in danger of doing.

However, the advances in science inevitably make demands on religions: faith needs to adapt to keep up with developments. Science seeks to understand the mechanics of life, while religions are concerned with the *meaning* of life. As our life and its cosmic context are changed by science and technology so to some extent does its meaning. The biologist Julian Huxley, the first Director-General of UNESCO and the grandson of Thomas Huxley, Darwin's friend, was aware of the need for religions to evolve and modernize when he wrote,

> The change in our conception of God necessitates the stressing of religious experience as such, as against belief in particular dogma, or in the efficacy of special ritual. (*Essays of a Biologist, 1933*).

Paradoxically, this can work both ways. Albert Einstein, for example, once said that 'the cosmic religious experience is the strongest and noblest driving force behind scientific research.'this quotation recorded in an *Obituary* to him (*19 April 1955*) is not alone among his statements recognizing that there are kinds of 'religious experience' appropriate to scientists. In *What I Believe* he writes,

> To know that what is impenetrable to us really exists… is at the centre of true religiousness. In this sense, and in this sense only, I belong to the ranks of the devoutly religious men.

Admittedly this is a limited sense of 'religiousness', but it is a genuine recognition that there is something beyond our understanding that warrants not only – or perhaps, not even – our investigation, but also our respect. It is somewhat comparable to the pantheistic openness shown by Marcus Aurelius in the second century and to the respect for an unseen power maintained by the deists of the seventeenth and eighteenth centuries whose Supreme Being did not intervene in the universe and was known through natural religion rather than by revelation.

Marcus Aurelius had acknowledged the existence of an impenetrable mystery, sometimes invoking it as 'the great harmony of the world', sometimes as Nature itself. Its operation was both within us and outside of us as an all-embracing mental force. The Greek philosopher Plotinus had expressed a similar insight three centuries earlier when he said that, 'to know the Divine Mind, we must study our own soul when it is most god-like'. Plotinus concludes that when this state is reached:

> Those divinely possessed and inspired have at least the knowledge that they hold some greater thing within them, though they cannot tell what it is; from the movements that stir them... they perceive the power, not themselves, that moves them...
>
> (Quoted from Bertrand Russell: *History of Western Philosophy*, p.313)

Mystery and poetry

Matthew Arnold, somewhat similarly described God as 'the Power, not ourselves, that makes for righteousness'. He was convinced that we experienced this Power, although it remained finally a mystery beyond precise description. He deplored the way theologians discussed dogmatic concepts, such as the Trinity, as though they were verifiable scientific terms and ridiculed the nit-picking sophistry of these 'able men with uncommon talents for abstruse reasoning' about the 'essence', 'consubstantiality', etc, of the divinity because (he wrote):

> ... in truth, the word 'God' is used in most cases as by no means a term of science or exact knowledge, but a term of poetry and eloquence... *thrown out,* so to speak, at a not fully grasped object of the speaker's consciousness, a *literary term*, in short; and mankind mean different things by it as their consciousness differs. (*Literature and Dogma, 1873, p.9*)

More recently, Karen Armstrong describes in *The Spiral Staircase* her experience of changing from the dogma-controlled life of a nun to a secular life of open scholarship. After this change she reaches the same conclusion as Matthew Arnold – that 'rational analysis' is useless for discussing God, since God is not an 'objective fact' in the sense that the data of medicine and science are (p.329). The study of English literature at university brought her to the same realization as Arnold that 'theology, like religion itself, was really an art form'. (p.323)

Gandhi, who like Karen Armstrong, was familiar with a considerable diversity of sacred texts, clearly considered God as a mysterious presence that cannot be pinned down. In *Young India* (1925) he wrote that 'God is that indefinable something which we all feel but which we do not know' before listing a whole range of attributes including Truth, Love, ethics, fearlessness, the source of light and life and conscience. He even suggests that God is 'the atheism of the atheist' – no doubt out of respect for the atheist's determined search for Truth. God 'transcends the purest speech and reason', he continues. He 'is a personal God to those who need His touch'. He is 'long suffering, and patient but…also terrible'; and He is both 'the greatest democrat', yet 'the greatest tyrant'. Finally He eclipses humanity because: 'We are *not* He alone *Is'*.

Gandhi's approach to divinity, like that of Marcus Aurelius, might sound like muddled thinking. But I think that their approach from every angle stemmed from their unwillingness to be dogmatic: they felt that there was no simple way of pinning down the inexpressible. Yet, despite the diversity of their reflections around the mysterious source of the power they drew on, they both showed a singleness of purpose in *using* it that led to considerable and positive achievement in their respective political pursuits. Although I have the utmost respect for both Marcus Aurelius and Gandhi, I think that when you mass too many miscellaneous attributes together to define the divinity they tend to cancel each other out. To my mind, the expression 'the Power we live by' underlies all the elements proposed by both.

The Power we live by is easily *recognised*. I need it to see the computer screen in front of me; I use it as I think what I am going to write; I can only press down the keys of the keyboard by virtue of the power surging through my fingers. Whether what I write is true or false, useful or useless is judged by that power, either by my conscience or by its influence or outcome beyond me. Nothing happens in a vacuum: everything either comes from that power or contributes to it. And yet it remains a mystery. Its ultimate source is not Higgs Boson – interesting though that phenomenon proves to be. We can neither analyse the Power in a test-tube nor bully it with prayers. But we can experience it. In fact, we cannot help experiencing it because we are drawing on it every second of our lives, though we are not necessarily *aware* of it. That requires concentration and attention.

There are so many ways in which the faithful seek to communicate with God and a lot of them are active rituals involving prayers, preaching, worship and sacrificial procedures. But ironically it was like the Anglican theologian, Richard Hooker, that the dissenting George Fox also found that 'our safest eloquence concerning (God) is our silence' when he founded the Society of Friends in the late 17th century. Quakers, as they became known, prefer to 'wait on God' in silence when they come together in their meeting-houses. Their assemblies are like spiritual oases from the noise and clatter of everyday life. They are prepared to wait in attentive silence for an hour if necessary; but generally the silence is broken at intervals by participants who may feel moved to offer some brief 'ministry'. They believe that the 'still small voice' of conscience or commitment is most likely to surface in an atmosphere of quiet contemplation. It is no accident that Quakers who worship largely in silence are also deeply concerned with peace in all its aspects from personal to social and political. It is only natural that people sometimes feel the need to escape from the hurly-burly of life for a moment of 'peace and quiet' – those two elements that belong together just as 'noise and war' are partners. In his play, *Henry V*, Shakespeare contrasts times of 'peace… modest stillness and humility' with those when 'the blast of war rings in our ears'. It is customary for a roll of drums to accompany the firing squad at an execution. National servicemen are obliged to shout loudly when with fixed bayonets they charge at the stuffed sacks representing the current enemy. The Norse god Thor (of our Thursday) is the god of thunder and of war. Symbolically, and actually, noise goes comfortably with killing and violence, as quietness readily accompanies peace and respect for life.

It is in periods of silence, perhaps, that we can get close to the mystery of the Power we live by. Perhaps the Quakers in their hour-long period of contemplation can sometimes for a moment achieve, like the poet William Blake, the brief power

To see the world in a grain of sand
And heaven in a wild flower,
To hold infinity in the palm of your hand
And eternity in an hour.

It is to poets, rather than statesmen, that we more commonly turn for writings conveying a sense of a religious experience of the numinous.

I was surprised recently to discover an example of this in the autobiography of my former university Professor, Vivian de Sola Pinto, an extraordinarily gentle and scholarly man – well-versed in poetry and literature in general. He tells how as a young child he had experienced an ecstatic vision one spring evening while taking a quiet walk in a suburb on the outskirts of London. He saw, as he looked out 'in the glowing centre of the setting sun', what he described to himself as 'a shining city full of people moving about among wonderful coloured flames.' The following quotation is abbreviated in order to concentrate on his subsequent reflection of its effect upon him:

> I suppose my 'theophany' was what Jung calls a Mandala vision representing the archetypal human totality that exists in the depths of the unconscious mind. Whatever it was, it has certainly had a considerable effect on my character and mentality. Far more than any religious creed or philosophical argument it has given me the assurance that, whatever appearances may be to the contrary, there is some sort of divine reality and that I am in touch with it, and, indeed, in some sense, a part of it. (pp.51-53)

Perhaps a wide range of people experience something we can call divine – a sense of the numinous, a communication with something beyond themselves. They may not be able to, nor even want to, define the source of the experience. The Power we live by ultimately remains a mystery. For some people this is not enough; they need a feeling of certainty – a faith to live by. What exactly is 'faith' and how far can theological dogma help seekers? That is the concern of the next chapter.

CHAPTER FIVE

Faith and the X Factor

> *Faith is the substance of things*
> *hoped for, the evidence of things not seen.*
> Hebrews, 11.1, A.D. 60

> *Faith is believing something you know ain't true.*
> Mark Twain, Following the Equator, 1897

> *As a Roman Catholic, I thank God for heretics.*
> *Heresy is only another word for freedom of thought.*
> Graham Green, The Spectator 19/4/81

> *There lives more faith in honest doubt,*
> *Believe me, than in half the creeds.*
> Tennyson, In Memoriam AHH, 1850

What is faith?

I suppose an incident I experienced once in India is a rather extreme example of faith. It was the action of a Hindu three-wheeler taxi driver when he knew that my wife and I were very anxious not to miss our train at a distant station. Soon after setting off he stopped at a wayside booth to buy something. When he hung it up on the windscreen we saw that it was a holy amulet. From that moment he proceeded at break-neck speed to weave in and out of the traffic with redoubled confidence. For some distance he even decided to drive on the wrong side of a dual-carriageway because there was slightly less traffic on that side. Amazingly he got us to the railway station in time, so (in his view, at least) the amulet must have worked.

What does it mean to have faith in 'God'? The primary definition of 'faith' in the *Oxford English Reference Dictionary* is 'complete trust or confidence', and presumably for many believers this would be an appropriate description of their faith. For 16th century John Calvin, for example, 'Faith is a knowledge of the benevolence of God toward us, and a certain persuasion of His veracity.' For 20th century Pope Pius XI, (though probably also for most other popes) 'Belief in God is the unshaken foundation of all social order and of all responsible action on earth.' Both assertions imply complete trust, but Calvin's definition is from the point of view of the individual and the Pope Pius XI's definition – literally *ex cathedra* – is more a political statement concerned with controlling the behaviour of individuals in society.

However, even in biblical texts Calvin's kind of certitude is not always so evident. In the N.T. book of Hebrews we find the more tentative: 'Faith is the substance of things hoped for, the evidence of things not seen (11:1).' This is closer to the second definition in the same *Oxford English Reference Dictionary*: 'firm belief, especially without logical proof', and would probably apply to many faithful Christians and Muslims. For example, Christians are encouraged to set aside reason in their theological thinking and Muslims believe that unquestioning 'submission' to Allah is man's primary duty. (The word *Islam* means submission.)

For Voltaire, in the famous *Encyclopedie*, 'Faith consists in believing what is beyond the power of reason to believe.' This raises the question, 'What things beyond the power of reason are the faithful required to believe?' Is it reasonable to believe, for example, in angels and djinns, the Devil and demons, places called heaven and hell, a day of judgement, everlasting life, the factual truth of every word in sacred texts, the specific accuracy of prophecies relating to the future, miracles interrupting the normal course of nature, the Second Coming of the Messiah, and so on? And do twenty-first century Christians really have to believe that Pope Benedict XVI had the power he claimed to grant 'indulgences' to pilgrims visiting Lourdes in 2009? No doubt different believers will respond differently to each of these items – some accepting them all, others rejecting all, and yet others allowing different degrees of belief and methods of interpretation to each.

The 19th-century educationist, poet and critic, Matthew Arnold, in his controversial book *Literature and Dogma* (1873) sought to preserve the essential values of Christianity while ridding it of all that made it uncomfortable or repellent to the growing number in all stations of life who were in touch with the successful new developments in scientific discovery and thinking. Arnold recognised that people were beginning to have more faith in their own experience and in what could be *verified* than in what they were simply told by authorities – including politicians and the clergy. Quoting a passage from the Old Testament book of *Proverbs,* he selected the phrase *'righteousness tendeth to life'* (which I think can be fairly paraphrased as 'honesty and decency enrich our lives and those of others') asserting that such an idea 'has a firm, experimental ground, which the Messianic ideas have not.' He believed it made more sense to be decent for its own sake than to believe that good behaviour was important because it meant that we would one day 'stand before the Son of Man at his coming, and …share in the triumph of the saints of the Most High.'

This latter belief, said Arnold, had a different character altogether. 'It is a kind of fairy-tale, which a man tells himself' which no one can either prove or disprove. It is what the Germans would call *'Aberglaube'* (meaning 'extra-belief'). Whereas our word 'superstition' is now generally used pejoratively to mean 'a childish and craven religiosity'the German word *Aberglaube* means simply 'the poetry of life'. The problems arise when poetry and science are confused:

> Extra-belief, that which we hope, augur, imagine, is the poetry of life, and has the rights of poetry. But it is not science; and yet it tends always to imagine itself science, to substitute itself for science, to make itself the ground of the very science out of which it has grown. (p.53)

The religious leaders who, no doubt well-meaningly, devised the creeds and concepts of the Virgin Birth, the Trinity, the Second Coming and similar poetic doctrines, knew that such concepts were poetry, *Aberglaube,* to support the faith, hope and good behaviour of their flocks. But now that their flocks are much better educated and more able to understand poetry and symbolism, it is time for the leaders to be frank about the nature of these concepts. There is no reason to suppose that acknowledging the fact that most of our religious concepts are poetic constructs rather than historical facts would result in a sudden influx of vice and debauchery: it is more likely that the fast-emptying pews would begin to fill up again if there was less *Aberglaube* required from the faithful! We can, for example, love and revere the Christmas story with its star, its manger, shepherds and royal visitors without having to believe every detail. The story doesn't need to tell us exactly what *happened*; it tells us what the birth of Jesus of Nazareth *means*. St Paul in his letter to the Corinthians put the relative importance of 'faith' in perspective when he wrote: 'And now abideth faith, hope and love, these three; but the greatest of these is *love*.' Faith – or 'extra-belief' – takes second or third place.

Personal faith as a driving force
Surely the best, most reliable definition of faith is 'complete trust or confidence'. That is to say, 'faith is what one *actually* at heart believes, not something that we are told to believe, or think we ought to believe, or that society tells us to believe.' Faith as a pretence to believe something we don't really believe simply because it's required by somebody else's constructed *system of belief* seems to me to be self-contradictory. For that reason when, long ago, I became an adolescent choirboy I could no longer join in the reciting of the Creed in church. 'Faith' in the terms required by religious adhesion seemed to me to be a denial of one's true self.

There is no doubt that religious faith of various kinds and degrees has enabled many people to achieve great things for the benefits of humanity: William Wilberforce and others worked for the abolition of slavery out of religious conviction; Martin Luther King advanced the rights of racial minorities; Gandhi worked for peace, social reform and Independent India; Florence Nightingale advanced the practice and status of nursing; Elizabeth Fry worked for prison reform. The list is endless: great achievements in art, music, literature, medicine and a host of other fields have been sustained by religious faith.

Faith under test

Faith has also sustained multitudes of sufferers from illness, poverty and personal tragedies of various kinds. Many 'prisoners of conscience' from St Paul to Dietrich Bonhoeffer, Gandhi, Alexander Solzhenitsyn and Terry Waite (and others whose release Amnesty International seeks to attain) have leant heavily on their faith in order to cope with their deprivations. Of course, not all such prisoners survive as a result of conventional religious faith. The story of Edith Bone, a medical doctor who wrote *Seven Years Solitary* (U.K, Hamish Hamilton, 1957) after surviving her confinement under the Communists in Hungary is a notable example. In her struggle against her captors, her faith in the fact that she was completely innocent of any crime and her belief that she belonged to 'a higher civilization'than her captors enabled her to maintain her spirits against barbarism and attempted brainwashing until at length she was rescued by insurgents.

Faith – as has already been mentioned in Chapter Three – is severely tested by natural disasters such as forest fires, floods, earthquakes and volcanic eruptions. 'How can a God who is good and loves his creations possibly exist?'

the faithful ask. Their leaders struggle with arguments to explain and excuse the God responsible. In response to the 2011 tsunami in Japan a few declared that the catastrophe was God's punishment for sins committed, but others argued that 'God was in the hands of those who helped the survivors'. The problem for the faithful arises from the fact that the 'God' created by theologians is credited with too much control over the universe. If, on the other hand, our God is simply the indisputable 'Power we live by', creating profusely and urging along the survival of all the life forms as far as is compatible with their complex inter-involvement, there is no problem to solve. The disasters remain a problem but the life force is innocent of them.

Dangers of Unexamined Faith

Despite its potential for good, faith misunderstood or misapplied has at least an equal potential for harm. Socrates, long ago, declared that 'the unexamined life is not worth living' (*v. Plato, Apology, 38a)*. Surely the same is true of the 'unexamined *faith'*.

History is replete with examples of violence and cruelty within and between religions: the 'Holy' Crusades, the 'Holy' Inquisition, the burning of witches and 'heretics', the burning of Catholics by Protestants (and vice versa). In more recent times we have seen the violence between Hindus and Moslems at the Partition of India (and before and since that debacle); the prolonged futile destruction between Palestinian Muslims and Israeli Jews (both seeking to guard what they regard as their rightful territory); intolerance and injustice shown worldwide to religious minorities; control of, and violence to, women; and a host of other problems and catastrophes arising from bigotry and prejudice – from 'unexamined faith'. Of course, there is frequently an unholy mixture of politics with faith in these instances, but the blend is often too subtly intertwined to be easily unravelled.

It is not surprising that many people think religion is divisive and tends to cause more harm than good. In a recent lecture, Professor Jagdish Gundara of the University of London Institute of Education, whose work involves him continually coping with multi-faith issues, pointed out that 'religions are by definition dividers... If religion is a "uniter" of peoples globally [they] would not need to work to foster inter-faith understandings and ecumenical work.'

Most of the problems relating to 'faith' issues stem from the intentional or unintentional 'brainwashing' of the young. To encourage children to accept concepts unquestioningly goes completely against nature. Children need to ask questions and they deserve to be given honest answers. They enjoy myths, fables, fairy stories (just as they enjoy Father Christmas), and in the early stages accept them as stories for the simple pleasure of make-believe. But as soon as they start asking 'Is it true?'they want to know if these things belong in the world of solid fact. To find their way in the real world they need to know whether these narratives are actual, verifiable, historical material or imaginative stories telling 'a kind of truth' but not factual. Most children are capable of this distinction quite early on, when in fact they begin the 'Is it true?' questions. I find the idea of teaching catechism, with ready-made answers that must be accepted unquestioningly, appalling. Fortunately, in the U.K. and in France, to my knowledge, religious education is much less taught in this way than it used to be. I agree with Dawkins that 'children should be taught not so much *what* to think as *how* to think.' But where closed-minded teaching still exists, in one form or another, it encourages unthinking orthodoxy or fundamentalism which can all too often give rise to fanaticism. Martyrs generally are so certain of a future reward that they are prepared to sacrifice their lives (and unfortunately those of their victims) in *this* world.

Perhaps a note on faith and martyrdom is necessary here. Thomas More was martyred in 1535 'in and for the faith of the Holy Catholic Church' (as he declared on the scaffold). William Tyndale, martyred a year later, was a Protestant reformer strangled and burnt at the stake for translating the Bible into English. Before and since these two, many thousands of brave souls have been martyred for peacefully standing up for their respective personal beliefs. I have a copy of a letter written to his mother by a Japanese *kamikaze* pilot just before setting out on his fatal mission. The writing is remarkable for the courage and sensitivity it exhibits. Clearly this pilot had absolute faith in the value of his mission. Sadly it was, unlike the missions of More and Tyndale, negative and destructive rather than life-enhancing. (Ironically – although I don't say this to justify it – his fatal flight contributed to the attack on Pearl Harbor that brought America into WW2 in time to ensure final victory over the horrors of Hitler's fascism!)

In both Christianity and Islam martyrdom and pilgrimage have been significant features. Martyrdom is *dying* for one's faith; pilgrimage is travelling (or in an extended sense *living*) for one's faith. Saint Paul, Saint Catherine, Geordano Bruno and more recently, Mahatma Gandhi and Martin Luther King all died as martyrs. Bruno, was burnt at the stake by the church authorities for upholding the Copernican belief that the earth went round the sun! All the martyrs in this selection could be said also to be *pilgrims* for going 'all the way' with their faith, not seeking death, but accepting it in their pursuit of truth. The Islamist suicide bombers causing mayhem today, on the other hand, may be brave, but their activity is totally different from that of the martyrs just listed.

Like the *kamikaze* pilots, their intention is personal glory or 'salvation' at the expense of the maximum destruction of other lives. Death-dealing 'martyrdom' is a far cry from dying for a life-enhancing or a truth-enhancing cause.

Fortunately, most followers of particular faiths don't seek martyrdom. We have to be careful to recognize that in every religious community there exist different kinds and expressions of faith. In a recent *Guardian* article (2.5.13) Mohin Hamid reminds us that,

> There are more than a billion variations of lived belief among people who define themselves as Muslim – one for each human being, just as there are among those who describe themselves as Christian, or Buddhist, or Hindu.

Mostly, they have not 'chosen'their religion; they are born into it, so they each 'evolve their own relationship with it, their own individual view of life, their own micro-religion, so to speak'. There would be less 'Islamophobia', he writes, if people would remember that 'Islam is not a monolith'.

Dangers of absolute certainty

Absolute certainty that one is right and 'doing God's will' leads all too easily to suicide bombers on the one hand or to self-righteous 'crusades' on the other. The disastrous 'war against terror' in Iraq has simply fomented more terrorism in response to the bombing and destruction by the self-righteous 'good guys'. On the other hand the Islamist 'madrassas' have produced more would-be 'martyrs' convinced that the destruction of innocent civilians is Allah's will. Meanwhile there are some ultra-orthodox Jews convinced that God has granted them alone the sole rights to a particular plot of land in perpetuity.

Jacob Bronowski, in *The Ascent of Man,* pleads against the destructiveness of 'monstrous certainty'. The fine ideals of communism suffered from absolutism, as did the less acceptable beliefs of fascism. Our knowledge is necessarily limited and relative. Bronowski believed we should adopt 'the Principle of Uncertainty', or Tolerance:

> There is no absolute knowledge. And those who claim it, whether they are scientists or dogmatists, open the door to tragedy. All information is imperfect. We have to treat it with humility. That is the human condition; and that is what quantum physics says... literally. (p.353)

The changes in our knowledge of matter, life and the cosmos over the past century have been phenomenal. Yet at each stage, it seemed that what was known was for most purposes adequate. In many fields, communications, genetics, etc, the next phase could scarcely have been imagined. And I am here referring to our 'known' physical world. Yet many theologians have seemed to think that they had an accurate knowledge of the spiritual world, pronouncing on the nature of God as though such knowledge was simple and self-evident. It is clear that there are many problems in the way of humankind having a clear understanding of God's nature.

For the sake of argument, let us imagine a fly taking a stroll on our hand as we sit reading on a warm day. We can assume that the fly is equipped with five senses – hearing, seeing, smelling, tasting and touching. What is extremely difficult to imagine, however, is what the fly makes of a human being, its temporary host. It can have very little idea (in our terms) of our overall shape, our features, modes of existence or locomotion. It can certainly not enter into our thoughts. We are bound to recognize a huge gulf separating a fly's perception from our own, although we are both creatures. How much greater must the gulf be between ourselves as creatures and the Creative Power responsible for our existence. I am not suggesting we cannot commune with the Power – seek to identify with it, to be 'in tune' with it – but I cannot claim to *describe* it adequately, any more than a fly could describe *me*. We have to accept that this Power, despite the efforts of theologians over the centuries, remains a total mystery to us – its ultimate nature is inaccessible to limited human perception and language.

Orthodox doctrines and heresies:the work of committees

The temporary 'definitive' forms of religious texts, doctrines, rituals, institutions and ethical codes are necessarily the results of decisions by committees (mostly committees of *men*) usually heavily influenced by the most charismatic members. It seems extraordinary that, as the various principle religions have evolved, these authorities have had the nerve to declare their particular orthodoxies the absolute, sacred truth. Having reached their doctrinal conclusions, those disagreeing with their construction were (and sometimes still are) declared 'heretics', 'unbelievers', 'infidels' or 'apostates' and treated as outcasts and criminals deserving vile punishments in the name of a 'loving', 'just' or 'merciful' God. In the first six centuries of Christianity the church declared some fifty different conceptions of the divinity to be heretical – Gnostics, Manicheans, Marcionites, Arians, Apollinarians, Pelagians, Nestorians and many others – all deviants were punished severely.

Later, in the Middle Ages, the Albigensian, Waldensian and other heretics in their turn were persecuted under the Inquisition. The torture and burning of free-thinking individuals was routine. After 'questioning', victims were burnt at the stake, because the shedding of blood by the church was forbidden. Ironically, these ritual executions were known by the Portuguese term *auto-da-fes* meaning 'acts of faith'. In our own days, similar 'absolutism' is seen in violent 'crusades' by arrogant western powers, and *fatwas* and ritual punishments, such as lapidation and flagellation, by fundamentalist Muslims convinced that their punitive 'acts of faith' are in accordance with the will of Allah.

By leaning on fundamentalism – the strict maintenance of traditional, orthodox, or ancient beliefs or doctrines – the anxious seeker demonstrates his or her cultural identity. Fundamentalism seeks to cement in-group relationships and keep society 'on the straight and narrow'. Unfortunately, although 'going straight' is generally considered a good thing, a 'narrow'society is not necessarily a healthy one. Because an idea or custom is traditional or ancient is no proof of its value in different times and situations. The major religious prophets themselves saw this. Fundamentalists seem to forget that Isaiah, Jesus and Mohamed are all revered because of the *changes* they advocated and brought about in thought and behaviour to meet the needs of their time.

Danger of 'Creationism' and 'Intelligent Design'

The fundamentalists who preach 'Intelligent Design' and 'Creationism' based on the account of creation in Genesis are among those who want 'certainties' and take the easy option, believing that something must be true in every sense because it's in the Bible and must have God's stamp on it. Unfortunately, their failure to understand poetry in sacred literature deprives them both of the beauty and originality of the Creation myth in Genesis and of the value and grandeur of Darwin's explanation of creative evolution in *The Origin of Species*. Dawkins rightly exposes the naivety of the creationists'stance from a scientific point of view. Their fantasies can be equally countered by common sense.

Do Creationists and proponents of Intelligent Design imagine a kind of person, spirit or whatever sitting for hours or centuries at a drawing-board (or perhaps on a cloud) carefully designing over 10 million species, often with minute differences, one after another – carefully sketching dinosaurs, amoebas, chimpanzees, pigeons, tapeworms, fluke worms, tsetse flies, carcinogenic cells, tumours and so on? And making drawings of the jaws, teeth and guts by which most of them can devour and digest the others? Even among the species that we find beautiful there is an embarrassment of subtle varieties. Why not design (say) just 100 different butterflies and 50 different dogs. The 'God of Creative Design' would be a great timewaster. (I know he'd have all the time in his world, but even so…) And why would such a creator purposely design most of them to kill each other? What a waste of celestial paper and ink, or heavenly computer software such designing would entail. And working under such pressure to get it all done in the 10,000 years the creationists' time-scale allows. All that designing wouldn't give the Creator much time for looking into people's hearts and answering their daily prayers. Such a vision of the process of creation belittles the Creative Power behind the universe.

Dawkins is certainly right to ridicule creationist thinking and hare-brained proposals that schools should adopt what they call 'Intelligent Design' as an alternative to the teaching of evolution. However, I think the Genesis story should be known as well, if only for its beauty and simplicity; but it belongs to the poetry or anthropology lesson.

Every religion has stories of the creation since time immemorial – they are the primitive but often beautiful attempts to make sense of the wonder of the world we live in and how it came about. But we now have a better understanding of the natural evolutionary *process* of creation that is even more wonderful than the stories, as well as being continually validated by one scientific development after another.

We do not need to jettison the ancient stories now; but we do need to understand their nature, as poetry and not as historical fact. Furthermore, if we understand the nature of

God in a manner appropriate to our own times, there is no need to invoke 'intelligent design' as a proof of 'his' existence.

Subtle Introduction of the Concept of Heresy

It is very disturbing that, because of misplaced faith in a totally literal interpretation of the Bible, a 2005 Gallup poll in America revealed that 38% of US teenagers 'believed that God created humans within the past 10,000 years'. (Apparently, even in England, an Ipsos Mori Poll [*Guardian Weekly, 13.11.09*] revealed that 'More than half of British adults think that intelligent design and creationism should be taught alongside evolution in school science lessons – a proportion higher than that in the US.') In one US school, Patrick Henry College in northern Virginia, all students, staff and employees have to sign up to a declaration of faith before they join including: 'The Bible in all its entirety (all 66 books of the Old and New Testaments) is the inspired word of God, inerrant in its original autographs and the only infallible and sufficient authority for faith and Christian living'. They must believe that Satan is 'a personal, malevolent being' and hell 'the place of eternal punishment where all those who die outside of Christ shall be confined in conscious torment for eternity'. Even in England, the head of science of Emmanuel College – a new City Academy – recently declared that in teaching science 'we stand firm upon the bare proposition that God has spoken authoritatively and inerrantly in the pages of holy Scripture'.

Employees of the new $25 million Creationist Museum constructed in Cincinnati have to 'sign a contract saying they believe in the Seven Days of Creation theory'. Adam and Eve and dinosaurs all feature together among the exhibits that span some 6,000 years – the calculation devised by Bishop Ussher in the 17th century based on the biblical account of the Creation. Man is portrayed as the *unique* pinnacle of Creation – unrelated to the rest of the animal world – and all the other creatures are there for his comfort and convenience. (The recent discoveries showing how DNA links us all are conveniently ignored.)

I have never understood the objection some people seem to have to our being related to other creatures. I find some animals more endearing and reliable than some people. And what other animals, given human skills and intelligence, would invent nuclear bombs, napalm, cluster bombs and other means of mass destruction devised by mankind to destroy one another?

Danger of Darwinism or Science as New 'Religions'

I have suggested that the 'faith' of Creationists is far-fetched. But the kind of atheism that has been called *Ultra*-Darwinism is equally ill founded. Belief in the theory of evolution is no good reason to reject the concept of God. It may mean modifying it. But then no two people have exactly the same concept of divinity anyway, and each of us gradually modifies our understanding independently as our experience dictates.

The Ultra-Darwinist atheists seem almost to have made a religion of Science with Charles Darwin as its prophet. Darwin, a true scientist himself, would certainly have been appalled at such a development. *The Origin of Species* concludes with the following famous passage:

There is a grandeur in this view of life, with its several powers, having been originally breathed by the Creator into a few forms or into one; and that, whilst this planet has gone cycling on according to the fixed law of gravity, from so simple a beginning endless forms most beautiful and most wonderful have been, and are being evolved.

In referring to the 'breath of the Creator' Darwin is inevitably obliged to use an anthropomorphic figure of speech, and it is true that his vision of the Creator may be very different from that of most of his contemporaries; but here is a clear acknowledgement of a Power beyond us by means of which all living creatures have their being. Darwin's genius was to establish by meticulous scientific observations a new view of the relationship between all living things. He had no intention of making science, which is a *method*, into a god.

We are now accustomed to seeing headlines such as 'The God Machine', 'Is God a Particle?', 'In search of the God neuron' which seem to equate 'God' with a *product* of physical or neuro-psychological science. Not far from Geneva thousands of physicists and engineers continue to work on the CERN particle collider. This 27km underground circular tunnel, built by the European Organisation for Nuclear Research, was 'designed to reproduce the incredibly high energies' believed to have been produced 'in the first trillionth of a second after the "Big Bang", which brought the universe into existence.'the experiment, which involved causing two beams of protons (minute sub-atomic particles) to collide at almost the speed of light, aimed to help us 'understand what the world is made of, and how'. Now that this process has found the mysterious phenomenon called "Higg's boson" we can better understand the nature of mass and we are closer to 'a Grand Unified Theory describing all physical phenomena in nature'. But can we claim that this is to "know the mind of God", in Stephen Hawking's phrase (*The Week*, 6/9/08, p13).

All this is very fascinating. Interestingly, much of it hinges on an act of faith that the Big Bang theory is the correct explanation for the origin of the universe. The theory, generally agreed by physicists today, argues that 'all matter and radiation in the universe originated in an explosion some 10 to15 billion years ago'. And 'thanks to theoretical and observational experiments performed in the last 20 years' cosmologists apparently 'now know approximately how the universe evolved down to about a billionth of a second after the big bang.' This seems to me an extraordinary pronouncement: a staggering assumption to be based on a variety of observations and calculations of other events at a vast distance in time from the event in question – the Big Bang – which is itself a theoretical concept. Although no one could disprove it, I cannot see that anyone can prove it either.

On the face of it the Big Bang theory doesn't seem to be much more compelling than Creationism or Intelligent Design. Of course, the Big Bang theory is scientific, based on evidence, while the Creation Story is poetry, never intended to be understood as fact. To cosmologists and physicists, immersed in their millions of zeros of macro- and micro- observations, the theory may be convincing. However, since by its nature the origin of the cosmos can never be proved by duplication in a laboratory, while the cosmic space-traveller may revel in it, the traveller on the proverbial Clapham omnibus may be forgiven for being sceptical.

Scientific Scepticism is Important for Science

I am happy to accept that our universe has been in existence for some 15 billion years, and our earth getting on for 5,000 million years. I live in a deep valley on the edge of the Jura mountains and I have no difficulty in recognizing that the marine fossils buried in the rocks high above my home didn't arrive there yesterday. But I don't have to take the details of the Big Bang theory as gospel any more than I have to take the Gospel as natural history. One is scientific theory, the other is imaginative poetry: neither can possibly be proved fact. Science is a voyage of discovery. Yesterday's paradigm had to give way to today's: today's paradigm must be subject to new discoveries tomorrow. When cosmologists claim *knowledge* 'about a billionth of a second after the big bang' (even 'approximately') I cannot help recalling the more moderate voice of the biologist J.B.S. Haldane who recognised that: 'The universe is not only queerer than we suppose; it is queerer than we *can* suppose it.'

In *Conflict and Man-made Environment (1991)* Vaclav Havel observes that

> We are still under the sway of the destructive and vain belief that man is the pinnacle of creation and not just a part of it and that therefore everything is permitted. (p.xxvi)

Ironically it is this 'vain belief', largely derived from religious scriptures, that fuels the arrogance of certain scientists to challenge the existence, or concept, of God. 'When Science has discovered something more,'they say, 'we shall all be happier than we were before.' Not long ago, apparently a new breed of scientific atheists launched 'an advertising campaign on the side of London buses, using the loopy slogan: "There's probably no god. Now stop worrying and enjoy your life."' (*Guardian Weekly*, 31.10.08).

Faith in science has brought a huge number of benefits to humanity; but it has also given us horrifying weaponry and overshadowing nuclear arsenals and brought us with carbon emissions, etc, to the brink of environmental disaster. Science has given us knowledge, and technology has applied it for good and ill. We need to recognise that faith should not be harnessed to knowledge alone but – perhaps even more importantly – to *attitudes*. As Karen Armstrong and others are pointing out:

> Faith is not supposed to be about signing up to a set of principles. Faith is something you do, and you learn by practice not by studying a manual... We need to get away from the endless discussion about wretched beliefs; religion is about doing – and what every faith makes clear is that the doing is about compassion.

Faith and the human brain

Unfortunately, faith is not always compatible with compassion. Thanks to studies by psychologists and neuroscientists we now have a better picture of how beliefs are acquired. We know – unsurprisingly – that beliefs (including prejudices and fears) are learned primarily from the prevailing culture. Kathleen Taylor, a neuroscientists at

Oxford University, suggests that beliefs are very similar to memories which 'are formed in the brain as *networks of neurons* that fire when stimulated by an event. The more times the network is employed, the more it fires and the stronger the memory becomes' (*Guardian Weekly*, 29.7.2005). In the same issue, using a different analogy, Peter Halligan (of Cardiff University) describes a belief as 'a *mental architecture* of how we interpret the world', built up, consolidated and crystallized from the fluid passing of perceptions as we experience them in our daily life.

These 'networks' or 'architectural structures' are crucial to our development. According to studies by Gerald M. Edelman at Yale, some 100 trillion connections between nerve cells in the brain are established during gestation and early childhood. (*Guardian Weekly*, 2.3.2007) Clearly, the mental structures formed in early life will have a powerful influence on the emotional leanings, faith, hopes, fears and prejudices of every individual. Inevitably, as far as faith is concerned, orthodoxy will be the default mode. The incentives for this include (or have included) social pressure, apathy, written and unwritten laws, the stake, excommunication, *fatwas* and so on. In totalitarian societies such as nazi, communist or other fundamentalist regimes, compassion is unlikely to be prioritized. When faith in the state or its leaders is manipulated from the centre, compassion often has to give way to survival. However, since compassion (or charity) is generally considered the real and practical aim of the principal world faiths – as distinct from abstract doctrinal or political considerations – this will be discussed under the heading of morality in Chapter 8.

Meanwhile, because the faith acquired by many individuals is often far from compatible with fact, it is necessary to consider in our next chapter some of the linguistic problems that stand in the way of clear thinking about 'God' and morality.

CHAPTER SIX

The silent X: linguistic problems

If spoken language is a gift from
the gods, writing is a human creation.
Sumerian dictum, quoted by David Crystal,
The Cambridge Encyclopedia of Language, 1987

We should have a great many fewer
disputes in the world if words were taken
for what they are, the signs of our ideas only,
and not for things themselves.
John Locke: Essay Concerning Human
Understanding, III, 1690

For the same things uttered in Hebrew,
and translated into another tongue, have not the
same force in them; and not only these things
but the law itself, and the prophets and the rest
of the books, have no small difference when
they are spoken in their own language.
Prologue to Ecclesiasticus, early 2nd century, BC

Language and divinity

We cannot really understand the meaning of the concept of God unless we have some understanding of the way language works. All our notions of divinity depend upon *words* constructed into definitions and descriptions that we have heard or read. Even today, when we are surrounded with books, most people in the West acquire their notions of God through the spoken rather than the written word. And looking back to the times of earlier theological speculation, until the Sumerians invented writing in the 4th millennium BC, speech was the *only* means of passing on information and ideas from one generation to another, and even then only a very few learned scribes could decipher the crude cuneiform symbols pressed into clay tablets. The sacred writings of all the religions depended upon this dramatic breakthrough. From the beginning of written texts there appeared to be something magical and mysterious about these recondite writings that gave the scriptures a special authority

The ability to record the spoken word was clearly relatively recent in the development of humankind. Nearer still to our own times the invention of printing brought scriptural material to a vastly broader public, a development incidentally fiercely resisted by the priesthood who feared losing their monopoly of access to the sacred texts. Perhaps their fears were justified. Spoken words are fluid, lost in the void as soon as uttered; but (as the Latin dictum recognised) 'the written word remains' – available to be consulted, interpreted and argued about!

Spoken language has been described as 'a gift from the gods', and in a sense it is. Like everything else human, language would be impossible without drawing on the

Power we live by. However, the power must not be mistaken for the product. The human language, which distinguishes us from all other living creatures, was not 'served on a plate' by divine intervention. It was achieved by the gradual refinement of the grunts, gasps, howls, yelps and other articulated animal sounds available, steadily allied to commands, perceptions, etc, and finally abstract concepts, as the hominids' brain enlarged towards that of *homo sapiens.* So speech is partly a gift, partly a discovery and partly an invention. We have shaped our languages from the raw materials available to us and we remain responsible collectively both for its glories and its shortcomings. We can be justly proud of the achievement of our forebears, but we cannot seriously blame God, the Power we live by, for all the anomalies, inconsistencies and ambiguities of language that create problems of understanding and interpretation.

The coming of language has its upside and downside. The downside is that it has separated us from the direct, intimate engagement with the environment that our earliest forebears had. All the other creatures sharing our environment have an unquestioning union with the Power that impels them. They accept their hereditary role and pursue it single-mindedly. Each has its specialities: moles are great diggers, nightingales sing, weaver birds make tubes of grass for their nests, and so on. For communication lions roar, ducks quack, bees buzz (and 'dance'!) and elephants trumpet. Although there is rather more to their communication than this, there is no questioning the fact that their 'language' falls far short of human communication with its vast vocabularies, its grammars, symbolism and so on. Clearly other creatures' physical forms and capacities, habitats, and limited creative imagination mean that they have very little scope for variation in their lifestyles and 'cultures'. Consequently they do not suffer, like humans, from what has been called 'divine discontent' – a nagging questioning of their identity and purpose.

The upside of the creation of language is that humanity has become incredibly inventive. Not only can we name objects and actions, pose questions and seek answers, warn, praise and advise each other, and order each other about; but we can even invent things that do not exist in the material world. Sometimes this is for fun (as in *Alice in Wonderland* or Disneyland) and sometimes in deadly earnest, because for most people there is a sense that the material world is not completely satisfying. The discovery or invention of a spirit world fired the creativity of our forebears. From finding spirits in rocks, trees, the elements and other creatures, humans began to develop whole cultures around devotion to divine spirits. The sun, the moon, the stars as well as ancestral worship all played their part. The same inventiveness that now produces multiple types of cars, bridges, music, buildings and typefaces was already at work devising multiple names and forms of gods. This upside, of course, has its own downside when cultures clash. In our modern global village it is difficult for some people to look beyond the bounds of their own faith-permeated culture in order to understand those they encounter with a different background.

God has no lips

It is generally forgotten that expressions such as 'God says this ...' and 'God says that...' are rhetorical or literary devices. God has no lips, no vocal chords, no lungs. A Power *beyond* speech, God is the source and nourishment of our life. It is men and women, the products of this Power who have lips and minds and an inner 'light' of consciousness 'switched on' from the moment of their birth. Language is a human acquirement; the Power we live by does not speak in words, but in acts. God's function is *creation*, not conversation. However, prophets and holy men have sought to understand the 'meaning' and 'purpose' of creation. Their glimpse of the wonders of our world and our existence and their enhanced awareness of our responsibility to revere and respect the miracle of life inspired them to communicate their vision to others.

The *New Testament* writer of the Epistle to the Hebrews begins his letter: 'God, who at sundry times and in diverse manners, spoke in times past unto the fathers by the prophets…' He clearly saw that if the Creator 'spoke' it was *'by the prophets'*, that is by human beings. What the prophets and other holy figures from Moses to Mohammad – including, Isaiah, Jesus, the Buddha and many others – communicated to posterity is usually described as 'revelation' (defined in the *Oxford English Reference Dictionary* as 'the supposed disclosure of knowledge to humankind of a divine or supernatural agency…') These charismatic leaders were not automatons. They were exceptional human beings, not simply taking down dictation, but applying their minds to difficult questions of existence. But their disclosures were sufficiently striking to lay the foundations of the religions and moral principles that have inspired generations of believers down the ages. We must beware, however, if in their enthusiasm they declare, 'Thus says the Lord…'this is rhetoric; what they mean is: 'This, in my understanding, is what God the Creator requires of us.'

Since I wrote this section I find that Keith Ward has written a book, *The Word of God? The Bible After Modern Scholarship* (2010), that also stresses the importance of understanding that the Bible is not a work dictated by God but a mixed selection of writings relating to the struggle of people in one particular religious tradition. Its value is not as an objective document of historical facts but as an important assertion of the existence of a 'transcendent spiritual power'.

No one understood the significance of these things better than Mahatma Gandhi, whose background drawn both from the cultural maelstrom of India and from so-called Western 'civilization' afforded important insights. In a lecture on 'Gandhi in the 21st Century', Bhikhu Parekh summarizes Gandhi's concept of God in the following words:

> God is infinite: the finite human mind cannot capture the infinite: therefore all our perceptions are inherently limited. Even if there is a direct revelation, that revelation is in a human language, with all its limitations to a human being, a particular human being, a prophet or whatever, who have their own limitations. (*The Gandhi Way,* No.94, winter 2007-8).

Of course, 'every religion captures a particular vision of human life', and many people cling exclusively and narrowly to the details of the faith they have been born into or pressed into believing. They fear that their commitment might be watered down by contact with other interpretations of the divine. But Gandhi recognised that 'every religion benefits from systematic and critical dialogue with god and with other religions' because this deepens, rather than weakens, our understanding of the infinite.

There can be little chance of achieving the universal harmony that the various religions seek until the faithful as a whole, not just a perceptive few, realize that religions – however inspired they may be – are *man-made* constructions, not divine injunctions. The Power we live by *enables,* it does not dictate. The realization of this important truth can come as a shock to some; but to many more it comes as a great deliverance. Things that jarred hitherto begin to make sense. There is no longer a need to experience a schizophrenic clash between one's scientific and spiritual understanding. Karen Armstrong, describes her emergence from the claustrophobic brainwashing of her convent experience when she encountered the idea for the first time in a scholarly theological work:

> I remember the extraordinary sense of relief I felt when I read…that our ideas of God were man-made; that they could be nothing else; that it was a modern Western fallacy, dating only from the eighteenth century, to equate faith with accepting certain intellectual propositions about God. (*The Spiral Staircase*, p. 327)

Words are not things

It is important to recognize that our various concepts of God are constructed, and that the words we use are not things in themselves but pointers to understanding. Take the word 'theology'. Put beside words like 'zoology', 'geology', 'mineralogy', 'hydrology', etc, theology sounds like another science dealing with solid facts. But all these other '-ologies' are concerned with observable matter – animals, the earth, minerals, water and so on – that can be studied by direct observation, weighed, measured and catalogued. The study of divinity is quite another exercise. Theology generally turns out, when we look into it, to be the study of a particular religion or faith construct, rather than the study of the Power we live by, which remains essentially a mystery. Theology is a creative, rhetorical and poetic exercise. Perhaps in some way, and in some hands, it is closer to 'astrology'than to the sciences dealing with solid evidence.

In his groundbreaking book, *Literature and Dogma (1873),* Matthew Arnold summed up the situation when he wrote:

> But in truth, the word 'God' is used in most cases as by no means a term of science or exact knowledge, but a term of poetry and eloquence, a term *thrown out* so to speak, at a not fully grasped object of the speakers' consciousness, a *literary* term, in short; and mankind mean different things by it as their consciousness differs. (p.9)

In the same book Arnold hazards two interesting definitions of God: 'The eternal *not ourselves* that makes for righteousness' and 'the stream of tendency by which all things seek to fulfil the law of their being'. Personally I prefer the second, which avoids the suggestion that human ethics are directly guaranteed by God. It is also closer to my definition, 'the Power we live by'.

Many of the problems faced by theologians and others attempting to define 'God' are semantic problems – the branch of linguistics and logic concerned with meaning. The study of semantics reminds us, for example, that words change their meaning over time. For instance, the word 'Lord' has a considerably different meaning in the 21st century from that in the middle ages or its equivalent in biblical times. A serf's relationship to his or her lord and master was one of total subservience. Today our attitude to a Member of the House of Lords could range from courteous or mild respect to toadyism, but we would not be in fear and trembling in the presence of one. Words also change their meaning according to the contexts in which they occur. The word 'Father', for example, means something very different according to whether our own father is a tyrant, a loving friend and adviser, or an absentee. It also changes in meaning as we advance in years from childhood, through adolescence to becoming ourselves fathers (or mothers) in turn. Yet both words, 'Lord' and 'Father', are used in theological and religious contexts as though they had simple, unambiguous meanings.

Not only do words themselves change, but times change around them. The *Zeitgeist*, or 'time-spirit' moves on, yet scriptural writings from far-distant antiquity are often read as though they still had exactly the same meaning in the 21st century. Human nature, it is true, has changed very little basically. We still have loves and hates, envy, fear and so on; but our knowledge of our place in the cosmos and of the evolution of life on earth and of advances in psychology, medicine, science and technology, have inevitably changed our understanding of each other and of our relationship with our environment.

Cultural lag and scriptural literalism

Despite a gradual move towards global uniformity, however, there still exists a significant range of societies from hunters and gatherers to tribal communities and democracies. The cultural lag between (and even within) these groups enables some people to cling to outdated practices by selecting antiquated scriptural authority in justification. The sacred texts of all the religions cover such a broad range of ideas and attitudes that isolated texts can be chosen to justify both worthy and unworthy actions. There is also the danger of interpreting poetical writing as factual prose.

Fairly recently I was sent a free copy of a book called *Bible Basics: a study manual* funded by the Christadelphian Advancement Trust. It is a very attractively produced paperback of nearly 400 pages. However, I was perturbed (among other things) to see on p.163 the statement:

> ... it must be understood that a ground rule of Bible study is that we should always take the Bible literally unless there is a good reason to impose a spiritual interpretation.

This seems to me to be a very unwise approach to scriptural material which is aimed more at spiritual nurture and enlightenment than historicity. Karen Armstrong wisely reminds us that 'we distort our scriptures if we read them in an exclusively literal sense.'she points out that there are 'truths' in sacred writing that are not the same things as scientific or historical fact:

> All the verses of the *Qur'an*, for example, are called "parables" (*ayat),* and its images of paradise, hell and the last judgment are also *ayat*, pointers to transcendent realities that we can only glimpse through signs and symbols.

The misguided terrorists who demean their Muslim heritage, concentrating on the idea of *jihad,* eager to slay unbelievers and become martyrs in pursuit of 'instant paradise and 70 virgins' are 'confused by inadequate understanding of the way scripture works.'

We can compare this kind of misreading with those fundamentalist Christians who imagine that the Garden of Eden story and the Creation story in Genesis were intended to be historical fact. They do a great injustice to the poets who conceived these stories. The message of the Garden of Eden story can be highly relevant to our situation today if sensibly interpreted and not read as history. For example, we can find in it a nobler expression of such truths as: 'where ignorance is bliss it's (sometimes) folly to be wise'; *or* 'unbridled knowledge can endanger paradise'; *or* 'the fruits from the tree of knowledge can have a bitter taste if unthinkingly exploited by unhealthy carbon emissions, wasteful nuclear arms races and unjust economics'. And the truncated seven-day Creation story reminds us that *we* didn't create the amazing world we live in but are guests here of a power beyond ourselves. It sets the evolution of the cosmos and our place in it in some kind of order; and it finally reminds us (and powerful or greedy employers!) that although we must work to survive and maintain our environment we need regular times of rest to recoup our forces.

Creative writing and imaginary worlds

In secular writing we accept that language is used to create imaginary worlds. We know that descriptions of Lilliput, Erehwon, Utopia, Wonderland, El Dorado and Hogwarts are fictions and appreciate that we can learn from the stories that take place in these settings without having to believe that they really exist. Why is it that many people encountering the Garden of Eden, Heaven, Hell, Paradise, etc, in scripture think that these must be real places? (Purgatory, a post-scriptural abode, incidentally, was added later as a sort of debriefing station. According to the *Oxford English Dictionary,* 'the name of Purgatory was first authoritively given to the Intermediate State in 1284 by Innocent IV.')

Then we have angels and archangels, the Devil and demons to contend with. Many fundamentalists would reject fairies and goblins as poetic fictions, yet regard the Devil as real. It doesn't occur to them, presumably, that personification is an artistic device, very popular in literature, particularly up to the middle ages, for bringing abstract concepts to life. Ben Jonson, the dramatist, and John Bunyan, the allegorist, later used the device to great effect. Why should the scriptures be different? It should be remembered that former generations tended to rely on poetry more than we do today. Before the coming of the written word, verse was the essential medium for remembering and transmitting information and stories from generation to generation. Early writing tended to continue this tradition.

Failure to interpret poetry leads to unnecessary complications. Take 'heaven' and 'paradise', for example. Heaven as a place makes very little sense. Where would you put it in the cosmos today? Would you hang it in the sky among all the technological hardware now launched into space? But as a *concept* heaven is useful. Most humans, one hopes, experience it briefly at some time in their lives. It is inevitably a subjective experience: everybody's heaven will be different – the suckling infant must be one example; moments of harmony with nature; sexual fulfilment; contact with exceptional music, painting, literature, etc. might each be heaven to different people. Many people must experience 'hell' at some time in their life: at moments of loss and despair, rejection or imprisonment. Guantanamo Bay and Abu Ghraib must have been hell to the prisoners (although perhaps 'heaven' to sadistic interrogators?).

So far I have stressed the poetic nature of scriptural writing. However, many sacred texts embody a mixture of poetry, history, legend, myth, legislation, counsel and prophecy. The difficulty is often to recognize which is which. Our standards of historical writing today are much stricter than in the periods when most of the sacred books were written. Accurate dating is now expected, and legend, myth and fact are nowadays clearly distinguished. The fact that these were not the objectives of the scribes of the Old and New Testaments of the Bible, the *Qur'an,* the *Bhagavad-Gita* and so on means that we need to adopt a certain tact in interpreting the different elements. In the first book of Samuel, for example, we are told 'Saul hath slain his thousands, and David his ten thousands' we are not looking for accuracy of body count but for praise of the heroic David. This is the language of legend rather that news reporting. Incidentally, we may well ask ourselves questions about the ethical content of the information.

When we read in Genesis the story of the Great Flood, we have to distinguish the mythical and moral elements from the distant historical event that almost certainly gave rise to the story. We don't need to get too worried about the logistics of loading the multitudinous creatures in the ark. The problem of pairing off the thousands of varieties of flies, ants and beetles, etc, is not part of the moral of the story! The story is essentially about justice, loyalty, obedience and, finally, hope.

Prophecy: insight or prediction?

Another problem we face interpreting scriptural writing is the issue of prophecy. Most people take this to mean *prediction*. It is true that Jesus of Nazareth seems to have come to see his role as the fulfilment of certain prophetic expectations of the Jewish people. This is not surprising, given the cultural and political environment of his time. But today it is unreasonable to put all one's faith in God or Jesus on what appears to be the fulfilment of various prophecies in the Old Testament. There are surely better reasons for trusting the Power we live by, or following the teaching of Jesus, than relying on a sort of protracted conjuring trick. Would a Creator and driving force of the cosmos really thread a series of obscure clues along a historical time-scale like a detective novelist plotting the way for a hero to finally solve all the problems? I find it grossly inappropriate and demeaning to equate the Creative Power with a kind of magical entertainer. As a long-term member of the Magic Circle I have frequently witnessed amazing and brilliant so-called 'predictions' and 'miracles' performed by colleagues. But I would hate to feel that my religious and spiritual life was based on such slender foundations.

The greatness of the Old Testament prophets was their courage in speaking out, attacking injustice in high places and warning their contemporaries of the likely consequences of their vices. They were concerned with present wrongs of their time, not far-distant future 'predictions'. Of course, by hindsight we can match up words relating to one event with a future circumstance by means of a little semantic juggling. But this is essentially wish-fulfilment.

In any case, the value of the life and teaching of Jesus is devalued rather than exalted by seeking to validate it with predictions.

The final book of the New Testament, *Revelation*, is rather a different issue. Some fundamentalist theologians struggle with the symbols and cryptic numbers to find prophesies in it relating specifically to our current or future situation, but they are wasting their time. Current scholarship dates the writing of *Revelation* at about A.D. 90-96 during the reign of the emperor Domitian. It was intended to comfort and encourage the suffering Christian community when Domitian launched a violent persecution against the Church because of the refusal of Christians to recognize him as divine.

The book is a call to all Christians to resist this blasphemous superstition to the death, coupled with the promise of life beyond martyrdom in the glory of God's presence. (William Neil, *Bible Companion*)

It could be described as a kind of call to non-violent *jihad* in the face of injustice. Its wild, apocalyptic visions reflect the state of desperation felt by the writer.

Faith and Miracles

Besides citing prophetical predictions to 'prove'the divinity of Jesus of Nazareth, *miracles* feature heavily as evidence in the *New Testament* and other sacred writings. This is not surprising in texts produced in a pre-scientific age when miracles – signs and wonders – were the common 'explanation' of inexplicable events. But by the 19th century sceptical people were naturally beginning to question the idea of using miracles as proofs of divinity. Matthew Arnold, in *Literature and Dogma,* noted how proponents of one faith were inclined to defend the 'miracles' affirmed in their own sphere while rejecting those of other beliefs. He believed, however, that

> To pick Scripture miracles one by one to pieces is…an unprofitable [task]… And yet the human mind is assuredly passing away, however slowly, from this hold of reliance; and those who make it their stay will more and more find it fail them, will more and more feel themselves disturbed, shaken, distressed and bewildered.
>
> For… the Time-Spirit… is sapping proof from miracles. Whether we attack them, or whether we defend them, does not much matter. The human mind, as its experience widens, is turning away from them. And for this reason: *it sees, as its experience widens, how they arise.* (p.96)

A sensible understanding of 'miraculous'scriptural stories appropriate to the 21st century is not helped when they are represented visually. Artists through the ages have inevitably added a visual dimension to the communication of scriptural events, stories and concepts. There is a vast range of often beautiful and inspiring religious paintings from early icons to the works of Michelangelo and William Blake But the use of visual symbolism can be confusing, particularly to a young mind. As a small child I believed that holy persons such as saints actually had haloes on their heads, that God looked like a huge old man with a beard, and (for a brief spell after going to a Sunday school) that a black Devil with horns and a tail might be after me if I didn't behave. Such paintings as the graphic descriptions of Hell by Hieronymus Bosch and others are not particularly helpful in forming a positive attitude towards the human condition and prospects. When in films, moreover, motion is added to visual images, a literal representation of scriptural miracles can do more harm than good to our understanding. I am thinking particularly of films such as Cecil B. De Mill's *The Ten Commandments* where, for example, the crossing of the Red Sea is depicted as a divine conjuring trick, scarcely appropriate for today's less credulous (we hope) audiences.

Whether by accident or design, we gradually build up our conceptions of saints, prophets, gods, holy places and imaginary environments. To a great extent the quality of our spiritual life depends upon the nature of the visual and aural poetry that we encounter. This leads us to our next chapter exploring the function of anthropomorphism in our religious understanding.

CHAPTER SEVEN

The Human Face of X – Anthropomorphism

Man never knows how anthropomorphic he is.
Goethe, 1749-1832: Maximen und
Reflexionen Werke, Weimar, 1907

But the reason why men have not a knowledge
of God as clear as that which they have of common
notions is that they cannot imagine god as they
can imagine bodies, and because they have attached
the name of God to the images of things
they are accustomed to see.
Baruch Spinoza, Ethics, 1677

And God said let us make
man in our image, after our likeness.
Genesis, 1.26

The anthropomorphic tendency

In the Old Testament book of Genesis we are told that 'God said let us make man in our image, after our likeness.' But the writer of Genesis might just as well have written: 'And *man* said let us make God in *our* image, after *our* likeness', because that is what has in fact happened through the ages. Even in the twenty-first century we can sometimes hear on BBC radio's 'Thought for the Day' references to God that summon up a picture of a bearded old man looking down on us from the heavens. It is natural for human beings to want some way of imagining – having a visual *image* – of any kind of phenomenon that interests them deeply. But the fact remains that – despite all the efforts of theologians, philosophers and scientists – the precise nature of the Power we live by remains a mystery. However, the 'bearded old man in the sky' image is not very helpful or appropriate for God in the twenty-first century.

Even nearly two and a half millennia ago the Israelites were wrestling with the same problem. Surrounded by idols that were worshipped as gods by contemporary rival faiths, they wanted to affirm a divinity existing at a deeper level than that of a material, man-made effigy. To avoid falling into the anthropomorphic trap they declared that God was beyond our imagination – he was simply *'I am that I am'* – not even to be named as humans are, but to be referred to by mystic letters – YHVH – a name too sacred to be spoken. (However, when speech cannot be avoided, YHVH is commonly pronounced 'Yahweh' or 'Jehovah'.)

Much later, in Islam, Mohammad was similarly concerned to counteract the anthropomorphic tendency. The *Qur'an* affirms that Allah is not to be depicted but his divinity is to be expressed through his works in the natural world. One result of the proscription against representing the divinity in human form was the general avoidance of representational art in favour of the development of superb creative calligraphy combined with beautiful natural and geometric devices embellishing so many Islamic books, architecture and other artifacts.

Despite such attempts as these to resist the anthropomorphic tendency, we find in Judaic, Christian and Muslim writing countless 'humanized' references to the deity. We' re told of the *hand* of God and the *heart* of God; we may be warned that God's *eye* is upon us, we should bow at God's *feet* or look upon the *face* of God. In addition to such physical expressions of divinity we find God endowed with distinctly human sentiments and attributes: God *loves* us, or is *angry* with us; 'the *foolishness* of God is wiser than men, and the *weakness* of God is stronger than men' (1 Corinthians, 1.25). Secular writers later continue the tendency: 'The Lord God is subtle, but he is not malicious' (Einstein); 'I cannot believe that God plays dice with the cosmos' (Einstein); 'God not only plays dice. He also sometimes throws the dice where they cannot be seen' (Stephen Hawking, *Nature*, 1975). The list of anthropomorphic references to the deity is endless.

Many people still today doubtless imagine (as in Cecil B deMille's film *The Ten Commandments)* that the fiery fingers of God engraved the Commandments on stone while Moses stood by. The anthropomorphic principle can play havoc with our natural sense of the way things happen. In this respect, the Islamic veto on visual representation of the godhead has much to recommend it. However, the symbolism involving the delivery of the *Qu'ran* by the intervention of the Angel Gabriel can also be misunderstood as factual. Religious leaders and prophets – Zarathustra, Buddha, Moses, Jesus, Mohammed – endow humanity with vital insights, example and leadership, but we must not forget that, however much these are divinely inspired, it is human scribes – usually a lot later – who put pen to parchment. It is natural and seemly that, given the time lag involved and the devotion of these disciples, the narratives become embellished. In the Christian tradition, the detailed Nativity story of the shepherds and the coming of the wise men is a case in point. The symbolism is clear: Jesus is worthy of reverence from both the powerful kings and the humble shepherds; but we are not obliged to believe all the details.

Anthropomorphism and Animals

Anthropomorphism, like personification, is the 'attribution of a human form or personality to a god, animal or thing' (*Oxford Reference Dictionary*). From the *Fables* of Aesop and others to Walt Disney's *Mickey Mouse* and George Orwell's *Animal Farm,* animals have been given human attributes to amuse and instruct us. On another level totem animals have been invested with spiritual significance among Native American and Australian tribes; and polytheistic religions have included important animal gods, such as the monkey god, Hanuman, and Lord Ganesh the elephant god among the numerous Hindu deities. When I have attended international conferences in India, a shrine to Ganesh is usually stationed at the entrance to the venue. He is a popular, much-loved, simple and accessible god. Indeed of the millions of the gods of the Hindu pantheon, it is Ganesha who is worshipped by all the sects. In practice too, it is Ganesha who is invoked before the commencement of worshipping other gods, as his blessings are considered auspicious:

He is the Lord of Beginnings, the benign Remover of Obstacles, and thereby occupies an eminent position...His one hand is usually raised in benediction, blessing the entire universe. Ganesha is the embodiment of success, good living prosperity and peace in life.

(Ganesha, KGM International, 1998)

To Westerners the revering of human-cum-animal divinities may seem curious. But I think this is partly because in our overcrowded cities we have lost touch with, and respect for, the natural world. The elephant in India represents power but also service to humankind. This seems to me very appropriate to symbolise our desired relationship with each other and with our environment. We seem to have a one-sided attitude to power in the West. The expenditure of our national incomes on power to destroy our enemies (a process euphemistically called 'defence') is vastly disproportionate to expenditure on power to create and serve our own and other communities. We could learn from Ganesha.

Gods, Humans and Supermen

Humans, it seems, cannot help investing other creatures and concepts with human attributes. This is true in both pantheistic and monotheistic cultures. In so many ways the gods conceived by humans are made to look like humans, think like humans and talk like humans – though on a superhuman scale. A linguistic problem arises in the definition of God as 'a *superhuman* being or spirit'. The word 'superhuman' has two essential meanings: (1) it implies something 'higher than man; beyond the capacity or power of man' (i.e. definitely *not* human), and (2) it evokes a heroic character, basically human, but *beyond the average* human capacity. Myths and legends abound in 'super-human' beings of the second type, from Hercules to Desperate Dan and Superman. In *The Myth of the Hero (1979),* the author, Bill Butler, observes that:

A distinction is often made in the study of mythology between heroes and gods, as if they were two separate kinds of beings. The origins of this fallacy may lie with the Greeks who paid different honours to the two classes. But even with some of the major figures of Greek myth, confusion arises; for Heracles and Perseus, to name but two, seem to have been accorded divine as well as heroic honours.

He suggests that a possible distinction could be based upon their functions: '...a god would be said to perform certain duties, the main one being that of creation of the universe, or the world, or mankind, or life, or death or whatever', while 'a hero would be one who battles with monsters, rescues maidens, kills the thing he loves, and goes on quests...' However, Butler continues, even these distinctions fall down because, 'too many gods are also heroes' and 'too many heroes are also gods.' He cites Marduk as a case in point. In the slaying of Tiamat, the chaos dragon, the chief Babylonian god was a hero; but as the founder of the laws and civilization of Babylon he was a god. Similarly, in the Old Testament Jehovah (or Yaweh), as the creator of Heaven and Earth, vegetation and all creatures culminating in mankind, he is clearly a 'god'. But when he 'demonstrates his powers to destroy as in the Ten Plagues, and his powers to work miracles as in the parting of the Red Sea', this is more in the role of the hero, avenging miscreants or rescuing victims.

This raises the question of man's relationship with the god-constructs he has created. All too often man's own aggressive instincts become component elements of the gods he worships. Jehovah, for example, is elsewhere known as 'The Lord God of Hosts'. The word 'hosts' here means armies. In this respect Jehovah is equivalent to the Roman god *Mars* or the Anglo-Saxon god *Tiw* (still celebrated, respectively, each week in the French word 'mardi' and the English 'Tuesday'). As I write, England has only recently quitted a war in Iraq and is still in Afghanistan, as part of a crusade against what President George Bush described as 'the Evil Empire'. We, the American, English and allied nations, are presumably 'the Good Empire' – fighting on behalf of the 'Lord God of Hosts'.

Warfare was famously described by Karl Clausewitz (*On War*, 1833) as 'diplomacy by other means'. In the present state of religious rivalry, we may well question the value, and fear the outcome of, this kind of 'diplomacy'. There is clearly a fundamental difference between 'armed crusades' and 'diplomacy'. Diplomacy implies the expert management of personal, social or international relations; and in particular it involves tactful negotiation. Diplomacy is essentially creative, armed crusades are essentially destructive. Whether we consider the medieval Crusades to the Holy Land or the more recent Iraq War, not to mention all the religiously inspired conflicts in between, the evidence is the same. It is ironic that religion and warfare are such close bedfellows. As Sam King points out in *Faces of the Enemy* (*1986*), 'It is impossible to think about the future of enmity and alternatives to war without beginning with theology. "God" has been the linchpin in the war system, the guardian spirit of tribes and nations, (and) the transcendent sanction for genocide.' (p.172) It seems to be the anthropomorphic god as hero (the power men die by) rather than the God of Creation (the Power we live by) that is promoted by nations. In Sam King's words:

> ...institutional religion has been a support for the ego and the ideology of society. The Lord of Hosts, the mighty man of war, has been the God of the realm – *Gott mit uns* – the God in whom we trust to keep our ramparts and economies strong. This God, the secretary of defense, has for generations been urging onward Christian, Jewish, and Muslim soldiers. (p.172)

Here 'God', anthropomorphized as 'the mighty man of war' leads nation after nation into conflict, each convinced that its crusade, war or 'jihad' is a righteous endeavour. For this reason I believe, with Keen, that a secular state is less likely to be led into war than one where church and state are closely linked. I share his concern that states need to show more commitment to environmental than to ideological issues. We still sometimes hear a rousing hymn composed in 1864 by the Reverend Sabine Baring Gould (music by Sir Arthur Sullivan) as a processional hymn for children:

> Onward, Christian Soldiers,
>   Marching as to war,
> With the cross of Jesus
>   Going on before.
> Christ our royal master
>   Leads against the foe;
> Forward into battle,

See, His banners go!

I certainly sang it with gusto as a choirboy during World War Two. The hymn *can* be interpreted in a metaphorical sense – as peaceful 'jihad' against the powers of evil (the anthropomorphized '*Satan*'s host' in verse two). But the vocabulary throughout – 'triumph', 'war', 'victory' and 'mighty army' – rather hinders an interpretation in the spirit advocated by Jesus of Nazareth. Hymns like *The King of love my Shepherd is* would seem more appropriate in a Christian church. I heartily agree with Sam King that we need to work harder towards becoming *Homo amicus*. In matters where understanding and negotiation are needed, we have failed so often even to be *Homo sapiens*.

The God 'X', the 'Power we live by,' is concerned with life – *all* life – not just specific tribes or nations. The routes to recognizing and revering this power can be through the highest, most positive aspects of the major religions: the message of peace and love of Christianity; the compassion and mercy central to Islam and the dutiful loyalty of Judaism. The smiling face of the Buddha, the reconciling influence of Sikhism, the concern for nature of Jainism – all these, and others have a part to play in unseating our former devotion to the gods of war.

Man in God's image

Returning to the quotation from Genesis at the beginning of this chapter, there is a sense in which mankind is part of God, or, as it were, a reflection of the Creator. We are in a sense – for good or ill – in partnership with the creative process, and perhaps the only witnesses and chroniclers of it.

Spinoza seemed to hint at this. Long before the word 'anthropomorphism' was coined (in the early nineteenth century), Spinoza (in the seventeenth) recognized the concept and its implications. Humans, he said, tend to 'attach the name of God to the images of things they are accustomed to see' – namely, human bodies. While suggesting that our anthropomorphic clinging to a physical visualization of the deity might be childish, he proposes that at the mental and spiritual level we ourselves are, nevertheless, inseparable from the Creator. He suggests further that 'the human mind is part of the infinite intellect of God'. On the *spiritual* level, he writes, 'we are partakers of the divine nature in proportion as we more and more understand God and conform our actions to His will'. From this perspective, prayer and the quest for divine guidance are not processes of reaching out but of reaching inwards.

Anthropomorphism and gender

Generally speaking, and normally in the western world, God is portrayed as a male. Grammatically it seems that he is always masculine: *le Dieu* in French, *Der Gott* German, *el Dios* in Spanish and so on. Although in English there is no longer a grammatical gender attached to the word, 'God' generally remains male in the imagination. 'Allah' for Muslims is likewise a male divinity. It is no coincidence that the scriptures are generally written by men, and in patriarchal societies. Matriarchal societies are surprisingly rare despite the fact that women play a much greater part in our individual creation than men. Had Jesus been born in a matriarchal society the Lord's Prayer would no doubt have begun: 'Our Mother, who art in heaven…' Had Jesus been a woman we would probably have had a female priesthood, forbidding men such privileges as serving at the altar. Had Mohammed been a woman, perhaps Allah would have been regarded as female and Muslim *men* would have to wear veils or the *niqab* to avoid arousing womens' lust.

There have of course been many female goddesses in the wider history of religion, certainly from the civilization of Ancient Egypt onwards, but there is no doubt that the three 'religions of the book' – Judaism, Islam and Christianity – tend to envisage the deity as masculine. The introduction of Mary the Mother of Jesus as a figure of devotion, notably in Roman Catholicism, was an important means of redressing the balance, but the Trinitarian God – the Father, Son and Holy Ghost – is clearly the primary divinity of Christianity and heavily masculine.

An interesting modern attempt to widen the Christian concept of divinity can be found in a best-selling American novel *The Shack* (2007;U.K. Hodder, 2008) by William Paul Young. It is an imaginative exploration of the healing of human suffering in the course of a direct encounter with God. When Mack, the estranged protagonist, arrives for this encounter it turns out that God is a black woman. In response to his surprise she says:

> For me to appear to you as a woman and suggest that you call me Papa is simply to mix metaphors, to help you keep from falling so easily back into your religious conditioning.

She explains that she is also known as Elouisa meaning 'the Creator God who is truly real'. In the room where this encounter takes place there are two other figures: one is Sarayu an evanescent being that we discover is the Holy Spirit and the other is a friendly carpenter who of course is

Jesus. This brief note doesn't do justice to the story of *The Shack* which as it develops involves quite a profound exploration of various fundamental features of Christianity including, of course, the vexed question of suffering and its relation to a loving God. I simply raise it here because of its introduction of a female God in the Christian context.

Deity with a human face

The mystery 'X'that is God, the Power we live by, lies at a deeper level than sex or gender. It is like the vibrant *kernel* hidden in the rugged nutshell. It underlies (and is often obscured by) the rough and ready intellectual constructs of the essentially tribal gods that we recognize. The fact that this God is without a human face creates a problem for humans that our anthropomorphic tendency tries to solve. The Christian concept of the Trinity was one such attempt to do this. Jesus had declared himself, like (half of) the rest of us, a son of God. (If he had said *'child'* of God it would have saved the declaration from the undertone of sexism that we now recognize.) In his prayer beginning 'Our Father which art in heaven...' Jesus clearly shows an attachment felt towards the Creator akin to that of a son (or daughter) to a beloved father. Why not therefore, thought the church fathers, make him *the* Son of God? By deifying Jesus, the church fathers linked an ideal role model to the godhead, making the Holy Ghost, the spiritual union between Father and Son, a third constituent. And so we have a god with a human face.

There was a value in this, but also a loss. The act of deifying inevitably distances a leader from his or her disciples: it is much easier to praise and worship a god than to follow a wise prophet's teaching and example. Perhaps

Mohammed's rejection of the concept of the Trinity was a useful warning; particularly as he didn't set himself up as an alternative god-figure to Jesus. Claiming simply the role and responsibility of a prophet, Mohammed kept himself closer to his followers.

To the extent that Jesus of Nazareth, elevated to the Trinity, was worshipped as God, he has been distanced from his disciples, and his value as a role model eclipsed. From the beginning of this phase, the flourishing of Christian statuary, both on and off the Cross, has been healthy for sculptors, but less so for worshippers who have tended to idolize Jesus rather than follow his precepts and example. The Hebrews, under Moses, had rejected idol worship – 'the offering of excessive or supreme adulation' to images, persons or things. In this way Jews guarded, and still guard, the mystery and ineffability of the Creator, the Power we live by.

There have always been human beings assuming for themselves a divine, or semi-divine role. In ancient Egypt many rulers regarded themselves as descended from the gods. Various Roman emperors declared themselves gods. The concept of the divinely ordered authority of monarchs was strongly defended in medieval times – particularly, no doubt, by those potentially in line for the throne. Later, the Divine right of Kings asserted by the House of Stuart in England continued this notion, as did the absolute rule of the Sun King, Louis XIV of France. Even in the twentieth century we have seen a somewhat similar attitude adopted by President George W.Bush, virtually claiming ownership of Space – the Heavens – in the name of America. Likewise, the hubris of the hypocritical holy club of nuclear states suggests that they feel that they have a unique divine right to possess weapons of mass destruction and genocide enabling them to stand in judgement over the rest of the human race.

Hero-worship and role models

Hero-worship is a natural human inclination and it is not surprising that there are those about who are happy to adopt the role of hero. There are, of course, 'false prophets' who set themselves up, or who are propelled by the media into fame and celebrity status and who lead their devotees (and others) into quagmires. The personality cults promoted by Hitler, Stalin, President Mugabe and Saparmurat Niyazov, the recent megalomaniac ruler of Turkmenistan, created various levels of chaos and disaster by their would-be Messianic leadership. On a slighter scale the celebrity status accorded to film stars, footballers, broadcasters and others in the public eye means that there are perhaps too many role models available today. Some of these provide excellent examples to their followers; others have too much influence in shaping the cultural ethos of their societies.

There is little doubt, however, that when it comes to morality – a close cousin of spirituality – humanity needs role models. Our behaviour is much more influenced by what we see, hear or read of other humans than by what we are *told* to do. The value of gods, or God, is to focus our innate sense of obligation and reverence. The value of laws, rules and regulations is to keep the wheels of society turning. But we are more moved to *behave* well by acknowledging the decency and courage of exceptional members of our species. Despite numerous distractions, Moses, Jesus, Mohammed and the Buddha are among the spiritual leaders who continue to claim the fervent allegience of multitudes of followers. More recently Gandhi, Martin Luther King and Nelson Mandela are among others whose example is positive, magnetic and sustaining. Such figures are worthy of our hero-worship because their life and work are life-enhancing.

Karen Armstrong writes interestingly about the 'myths of the hero' which she says 'are not meant to give us historical information about Prometheus or Achilles – or for that matter about Jesus or the Buddha. Their purpose is to compel us to act in such a way that we reveal our own heroic potential.' When she came to believe that faith was – or should be – more about ethical practice than dogmatic belief, she decided that 'Religion is not about accepting twenty impossible propositions before breakfast, but about doing things that change you.' The life-enhancing heroes we revere, she discovered, were independent; they did not waste their own lives, thoughts and dreams by slavishly following the crowd. If we seriously want to follow the heroic prophets and spiritual leaders we revere, we need to imitate their spirit of independence and not simply follow authority figures with 'unthinking acceptance'. Such behaviour 'may make an institution work more smoothly, but the people who live under a regime will remain in an infantile, dependent state.'

The persistence of heroic myths throughout the ages strongly suggests the human need for dynamic role models. Whether such 'model humans' function best as 'the human face of God' is a moot point. They certainly function well in their own right. There is no doubt, for example, that Jesus of Nazareth appeals to the atheist Richard Dawkins. He describes him as 'one of the great ethical innovators of history;' and among other things wrote an article called

'Atheists for Jesus'. Dawkins appreciated Jesus's independence of thought, as he writes in his book *The God Delusion*:

> Jesus was not content to derive his ethics from the scriptures of his upbringing. He explicitly departed from them for example when he deflated the dire warnings about breaking the Sabbath. 'The Sabbath was made for man, not man for the sabbath' ...Jesus has been honoured as a model for that very thesis. (p.250)

The Marxist intellectual Terry Eagleton is sufficiently enthusiastic about Jesus to have recently devoted a book to him (*The Week*, 5/1/08).

When both Dawkins and Eagleton – two prominent atheists – appear to derive most of their values at least indirectly from the kind of teaching offered by Jesus, this raises the question of the relationship, if any, between morality and faith in God. How far are our values dependent on a belief in God – as 'X' – the Power we live by? Clearly, all our actions are dependent upon this source, since nothing can be done without power. But whether this is used for good rather than harm requires direction and motivation. The next chapter considers these issues.

CHAPTER EIGHT

Morality and the X factor

*If God did not exist,
everything would be permitted.*
Fyodor Dostoevsky,
'The Brothers Karamazov', 1880

*There is no good case to be made for
our possession of a sense of right and wrong
having any clear connection with the
existence of a supernatural deity.*
Richard Dawkins, The God Delusion, 2006

*Ethical axioms are found and tested not
very differently from the axioms of science. Truth
is what stands the test of experience.*
Albert Einstein, Out of My Later Years, 1950

How Far is Morality God-given?

George Washington, in his farewell address on September 17th, 1796, offered the advice: 'Let us with caution indulge the supposition that morality can be maintained without religion.' On the other hand not long before, Alexander Pope, in his *An Essay on Man,* (1732) had declared:

> Know then thyself, presume not God to scan,
> The proper study of mankind is man,

suggesting that man is himself responsible for defining his ethical responsibilities. How far, in fact, does morality depend upon God, or belief in God's existence? Before seeking an answer to this, maybe it is worth noting that even *with* belief in God, virtually everything seems to be permitted, at least by some of the faithful. In fact faith itself is quite commonly used to *justify* acts that to many of us appear highly immoral.

In the past witches and 'heretics' have been burnt at the stake in the name of Christianity. More recently, Christian supporters of the 'Right to Life' movement have murdered doctors who have helped women desperately in need of abortions. Women have been murdered or had acid thrown in their faces by fanatical Muslims in the name of 'honour'. Palestinians have been killed and harassed by Zionists who believe they have a divine right to occupy the land where their Muslim neighbours live. Such wrongs, and many more, are justified as having scriptural, God-given, authority. In these three cases it is essentially the same God cited, but from misguided readings of New Testament, Qu'ranic and Old Testament scriptures, respectively. It does seem then that everything is permitted, providing you search for the particular texts that can be misinterpreted to suit your designs!

If, however, we take God to be 'the Power we live by', we go beyond scriptural texts to the power that underlies all three of the religions quoted, and doubtless all other existing religions. The Power we live by is not one of the many gods that we have created, but the God that has created *us*. It is this power, of course, that presumably provokes and certainly *enables* our quests for understanding the difference between right and wrong behaviour and for constructing moral paradigms. But when we consider it thoughtfully we may find that its operations do not equate precisely with what humans regard as 'good' and 'evil'. I want to argue that human morality is man-made, just as the diverse multitude of gods humans worship are man-made.

Take, for example, the commandment 'Thou shalt not kill'. I am enthusiastically in favour of this principle: as a pacifist I am against war as a means of solving problems; as a human rights activist I am against capital punishment; and as an admirer of Gandhi I am slowly veering towards vegetarianism! But if we look to the Creative Power for justification of this law, we find that every meal in God's universe involves the death and devouring of at least one other creature – animal or vegetable. Tennyson described Nature as 'red in tooth and claw', and John Stuart Mill characterized it as 'divided into devourers and devoured' with 'many creatures being lavishly fitted with instruments to devour their prey'. In terms of morality, when the mouse eats the grain, it's 'good' for the mouse but 'bad' for the seeds; when the cat eats the mouse it's 'good' for the cat but 'bad' for the mouse. When we eat a tomato we kill its potential to reproduce itself; when we eat mutton, we slaughter a helpless living creature. Moral terms – 'kill', 'good', 'bad' – dissolve into relativity in the Creator's ecosystems. Evidently we cannot justify our prohibition against killing by reference to the operations of the Power we live by.

Does the Power We Live By Love Us?

However, to judge by its productivity, it seems that the Creative Power 'loves' life, although it seems to be oblivious to death. We could almost say that, rather than telling us *not* to kill, the Creative Power commands us to devour, and so kill, in order to live. Death is simply the corollary of life. Life is a gift to each of us; living creatures must eat to survive; and devouring food is a pleasure as well as a necessity. In this sense we can say that the Creative Power 'loves' us – is concerned for our well-being – by ensuring a supply of living nourishment. This is potentially true for all the creatures on the ecological chain, so it is 'good' for them all – at least until they become victims for the 'good' of the next link above them! Even within individual species deaths are necessary to provide space for subsequent life. This principle is recognized in the *yin* and *yang* of Chinese philosophy: male and female, dark and light, 'good' and 'bad' are necessary complementary forces present throughout life.

We can of course argue that our moral values apply only within our own species: flies, cats or kangaroos, given speech, would each no doubt come up with a different set of values. But even within our own species, we may not necessarily agree on all ethical details. Most humans would accept that murdering another human is wrong, while slaughtering a sheep for food is acceptable. But a strict vegetarian or vegan can offer convincing arguments that there is no real difference between murder and slaughter. We now know, for instance, that we share a vast amount of our genetic inheritance with the cattle and poultry we imprison and devour.

It is evident, for example, that concern for others isn't only the province of humankind. Some inner impulse drives penguins to undergo considerable hardship in the interests of their young. Dogs frequently show extreme examples of loyalty to their masters. Even independent minded cats can show real affection as well as cupboard love. Among more exotic examples we find a 15-foot crocodile loyally attached for 17 years to the Cost Rican fisherman who had rescued him (*The Independent on Sunday,* 11.2.07). Recent experiments in the Max Planck Institute of Evolutionary Anthology found that chimpanzees

> will go out of their way to help others, without the prospect of reward' for example by 'helping a human volunteer trying in vain to reach for a stick through their cage bars... .the chimps spontaneously passed the human the stick – even when they had to climb over a 6-foot wall to reach it.' (*The Week*, 7.7.07)

Richard Harris, who was Bishop of Oxford, generously acknowledges that the atheist Richard Dawkins argues soundly about morality. He agrees with Dawkins that, however much humans may differ from other creatures, many animals share with us a capacity for altruism. Within their species, for example, 'mammals can act with great altruism on behalf of their offspring' and across species we find 'the reciprocal benefits that flowers and bees bring to each other through the process of pollination'. The former Bishop agrees with the atheist that 'Far from believing that we are always driven by considerations of narrow self-interest…Dawkins shows that it is just as built-in for mammals such as ourselves to act in the interest of others' (*Guardian Weekly, 4/1/08*).

When we take a wide view of the creative power 'X' in the natural world it is clear that we find ample examples of both tooth-and-claw behaviour on one side and altruistic cooperation on the other. So we cannot build our human ethics simply by reference God's creation. We have to look for the origin of human morals from what men and women have found within themselves and evolved between themselves.

The Principle of Reciprocity

Spinoza invokes the principle of reciprocity in his discussion of human morality. 'Men are most useful to each other who are mutually ruled by the laws of reason,' he wrote. 'They find by experience that by mutual aid and co-operation they can the more easily secure what they need.' This is clearly the kind of thinking that led Hammurabi, the Amorite king of Babylon, to create his famous Code of Laws in the eighteenth century BC. and led subsequently to the Ten Commandments given to the Hebrews by Moses in the thirteenth century BC. It is the kind of thinking that led in the Middle Ages to the formulation of the Seven Deadly Sins and the Seven Virtues. It is the thinking made possible by human empathy with others and epitomized in the Golden Rule: 'Do unto others as you would have them do to you'. By means of this rule self-interest is converted into social well-being: all benefit where each benefits.

Spinoza recognized that 'the power by which we preserve our being is the power of God, that is a part of His essence.' However, 'man is subject to passions because he follows the order of nature.' Submission to one's passions may not always be in a person's interest, or may hinder the well-being of others. Therefore we need some moral guidelines in order to direct our actions. Spinoza proposes several principles of which the most succinct and telling is:

> That which tends to conserve our existence we denominate good; that which hinders this conservation we style evil.

He reminds us that the terms 'good' and 'evil' are relative terms:

> Good is that which is useful to us; evil that which impedes the possession of good. However, the terms good and evil are not positive, but are only modes of thought by which we compare one thing with another. Thus music is good to a melancholy mind, bad to a mourning mind, but neither bad nor good to a deaf man. (v. Hammerton,p.177)

Since 'man is a social animal', Spinoza says, we are happiest if our actions are 'in harmony with our [shared] nature' and 'in harmony with the dictates of reason'.

> Hence, men acting in accord with the dictates of reason, desire nothing for themselves but what they desire for all. This renders them just, faithful and honourable (*Ethics IV: Concerning Human Bondage and Human Liberty)*.

Baruch de Spinoza's *Ethics* was not published until 1677, after his death, 'owing to rumours as to its nature and aims'. It was immediately proscribed by the states of Holland and West Friesland because it seemed at the time tainted with atheism and pantheism. In the present climate, it is clearly not atheistic, and the elements that resonate with pantheism speak more comfortably to twenty-first century's understanding of, and concern with, the total interconnectedness of our threatened environment.

Importance of self-knowledge

Spinoza's conclusion just quoted above is essentially a restatement of the golden rule, 'do to others as you would have them do to you'. If we go farther in examining this maxim it becomes clear that the insight behind the rule depends on recognizing the importance of self-knowledge coupled with a capacity for empathy. Understanding the truth about ourselves helps us to recognize the truth of others' natures and needs.

Nearer to our own times, Gandhi is an exemplary exponent of principles relating to both concepts. He believed that the quest for Truth – of oneself and of our relationship with others – was central to the solution of moral issues. Our actions must be based on a true assessment of every situation, but where the truth is too obscure or complex for certainty we must beware of false judgement and action. His advocacy of *Satya-graha* (literally 'truth-tenacity') was based on his belief in its power as 'soul force' – more powerful than weapons or punishment: 'It excludes the use of violence because man is not capable of knowing the absolute truth and, therefore, not competent to punish.'

This unwillingness to punish or hurt others stems also from the golden rule and leads to the concept of love:

One who hooks his fortunes to *ahimsa,* the law of love, daily lessens the circle of destruction, and to that extent promotes life and love; he who swears by *himsa,* the law of hate, daily widens the circle of destruction, and to that extent promotes death and hate.

These sayings of Gandhi, blending Hindu and Christian thought, are clearly in harmony with Spinoza's universalistic philosophy and with the concept of 'X' as the universal Power we live by.

The principle of reverence for life

The Nobel Peace Prize winner, Albert Schweitzer (1875-1965), like Gandhi, looked to both east and west in his theological and philosophical thinking. While working in the hospital he founded in Africa and making a study of the major world religions, he came to the conclusion that the essence of ethical and spiritual living could be summed up as *'reverence for life'.* In reaching this conclusion, he was particularly influenced by Buddhism and Jainism and by the philosophical writings of Schopenhauer which stressed the 'will to live' of all living things:

Ethics are complete, profound, and alive only when addressed to all living beings. Only then we are in spiritual connection with the world... Profound love demands a deep conception and out of this develops reverence for the mystery of life. It brings us close to all beings. To the poorest and smallest, as well as all others. We reject the idea that man is "master of other creatures", "lord" above all others. We bow to reality. (v. *The Schweitzer Album,* ed. Erica Anderson, 1965)

The attitude and practice of 'reverence for life' focuses on what is most important in Christianity, Islam and Judaism. It is also consistent with much humanist, atheist and agnostic thinking. Albert Einstein said of Schweitzer that, 'He is the only Westerner who has had a moral effect on this generation comparable to Gandhi's. As in the case of Gandhi, the extent of this effect is overwhelmingly due to the example he gave by his own life's work.'

Science and morality

Einstein was of course a scientist, but ethically and spiritually he is close to Gandhi and Schweitzer. 'For the scientist [Einstein wrote] there is only 'being', but no wishing, no valuing, no good, no evil; no goal'. His use of the term 'scientist' here can lead to misunderstanding since it puts the stress on the person rather than the activity. But a scientist is not only a scientist; he or she is also a human being with feelings, hopes, fears, a capacity for 'valuing', a recognition of the difference between 'good and evil' and a concern with personal 'goals'. While occupied with research and experiments he or she must concentrate on the *facts* alone to arrive at the truth, but outside the laboratory the scientist is free to evaluate discoveries in terms of their human and social implications. Elsewhere Einstein wrote '*Science* can only state what is, not what should be' – the facts. But as a person and moralist, he was equally concerned with 'what should be'. After his findings had lead to the development of the atomic bomb, for example, he wrote: 'If only I had known, I should have become a watchmaker.'

It is true, however, that for some scientists the distinction between the person and the activity becomes blurred. Science can become an end in itself – virtually a god. Human scruples can be lost in the devotion to new discoveries. Apparently Enrica Fermi, who worked on the atomic bomb, was among those totally fascinated by the splitting of the atom. 'Don't bother me with your conscientious scruples,' he is reported to have declared. 'After all the thing's superb physics.' (Quoted in a letter by Howard Rosenbrock FRS to *The Independent*).

William James (in the *Varieties of Religious Experience, 1902*) put the scientific position clearly when he wrote 'The God whom science recognises must be a God of universal laws exclusively... He cannot accommodate his processes to the convenience of individuals.' Such a god, I agree, will not overturn natural laws, nor show individual or tribal favouritism, but remain 100 percent reliably anchored in the nature of things that we 'understand', or at least recognise. Such a god is 'The Power we live by'.

The question remains whether morality is endowed by this Power, or acquired. The philosopher J. S. Mill who experienced a utilitarian upbringing was convinced that 'the moral feelings are not innate but acquired' (*Utilitarianism, 1863*). Charles Darwin, on the other hand, believed that 'Man... derives his moral sense from the social feelings which are instinctive or innate in the lower animals' (*The Descent of Man, 1874*). The likelihood is that both genetic and acquired elements are involved. The *capacity* for altruism seems to be genetic, the *specific forms* which such altruism takes, however, will be strongly influenced by the social and religious milieu in which a person grows up.

Morality and truth

For the (basically Zoroastrian) Persians under the influence of Zarathustra (c.1200 BC) *Truth* (as for Gandhi) was apparently the central pivot of their moral thinking:

'Lying is considered among them the very basest thing. And second, indebtedness, especially because, as they say, the debtor is bound to lie somewhat.' (From *The History of Herodotus*, translated by David Grene.)

It is curious that the Ten Commandments only touch on Truth obliquely (in the ninth commandment about bearing false witness against one's neighbour). Neither does 'lying' feature among the Seven Deadly Sins nor 'truth' among the Seven Cardinal Virtues of mediaeval Christianity. It is true, of course, that truth is recommended in the scriptures in the *Qu'ran,* in the O.T. Psalms, and notably in the N.T. Gospel of St. Matthew (5:37): 'Plain "Yes" or "No" is all you need to say; anything beyond that comes from the devil.' But the centrality of Truth to morality would seem to deserve more respect among the faithful than it has been given. When we think of the fate of Bruno, Galileo and many others at the hands of the Inquisition, it appears that Truth has fared better in the field of science than in that of religion.

The graphic biblical description of the Ten Commandments given by God to Moses on Mount Sinai (Exodus 20:1-21), while it has a vivid hold on the imagination, scarcely accords in detail with what we know about how laws come about. The writer of Genesis was not lying but, in the usual way of his time, employing poetry to impress upon the reader, or in most cases the hearer, with the importance of these laws to facilitate peaceful human conduct. In the final analysis the written laws and scriptures we receive – however noble – are inevitably man-made attempts to express the divine.

Zarathustra, Moses and Mohammed, each in his time, found themselves responsible for the leadership of motley and tempestuous communities of individuals with different tribal allegiances. Somehow, cohesion and discipline had to be established if they were to work together in peace. In such circumstances it was essential to institute rules and regulations, and for these rules to be regarded as sacrosanct (preferably by divine cachet) to guarantee obedience. In due course the myths tend to be sanctioned by custom and tradition and if the laws are good the details of their validation become less and less important. The obligations of strict Judaism and Islam remain very demanding, while the demands upon Christians have perhaps fluctuated more in their intensity according to times, places and sectarian rivalries.

Buddhism and Taoism exemplify 'religions' that are less invasive for individuals; they are less (if at all) god-centred and more in the nature of practical, and at the same time, mystical, philosophies. But orthodox Judaism, medieval Christianity and ultra-traditional versions of Islam have tended to put the collective before the individual – strict rules and dogmas being regarded as necessary to hold the community of faithful together. Obedience (including 'submission' in Islam) has held a high place in all these three religions. Unfortunately, once the collective is regarded as more important than the individuals who compose it, moral issues are blurred; the executive powers fear their loss of control and the dissolution of the community or state. The result of this is seen in

Inquisitions, *fatwas*, excommunications and so on. Failure to recognise that individuals owe loyalty to their own 'truths'too often results in much injustice and tragedy. The conformity demanded by the Taliban, for example – with brutal punishments exacted for non-conformity – is an extreme instance of this. Like Hitler's fascism and Stalin's Communism such movements eventually collapse; but not before they have inflicted great mischief on the states or communities that have suffered them. In the case of Hitler's rule there is not even a nodding concern for truth in his establishment of authority. In *Mein Kampf* he brazenly declares his contempt for his subjects:

> The victor will not be asked afterwards whether he told the truth or not ... The broad masses of the people... will more easily fall victims to a big lie than to a small one. (v. also: Shirer, William L: *The rise and Fall of the Third Reich,* USA, Simon and Schuster, 1960.)

'X', morality and life-enhancement

The Power we live by gives no laws, but if we look around at the natural world we find that its operations are positive and offer life-enhancing principles: survive, eat, drink, enjoy, reproduce, work, be active and cooperate. Compared with these observations it seems that the man-made laws of religion, strengthened by the divine sanctions attached to them, tend to be negative. For example, while the Ten Commandments have proved to be valuable guidelines, only two of them are positive: (4) observe a day of rest, and (5) honour your parents. All the rest are 'Thou shalt *not...*'

Despite the positive nature of the teachings of Jesus of Nazareth, a further negative element was introduced into the Judeo-Christian line of development by Saint Paul, Saint Augustine and Calvin who between them promoted and (over time) modified the doctrine of Original Sin. The final version of this doctrine is succinctly summarized by Bertrand Russell as follows:

> Adam, before the Fall, had had free will, and could have abstained from sin. But as he and Eve ate the apple, corruption entered into them, and descended to all their posterity, none of whom can, of their own power, abstain from sin. Only God's grace enables men to be virtuous. Since we all inherit Adam's sin, we all deserve eternal damnation.

This doctrine is far from life-enhancing, and when we add to it the notion of a loving God sacrificing his son to a cruel death in order to redeem the race he had previously allowed to be condemned to sinfulness we can understand how the 19th century Christian writer Matthew Arnold found the doctrine demeaning and totally unhelpful in man's pursuit of moral perfection.

Karen Armstrong's twentieth century reaction to the doctrine was similar. She describes her feelings about it soon after emerging from her life under conventual rules. For the first time in her life she had found the freedom to think for herself and to question the notion of God with which she had been force-fed. What kind of God, she asked herself,

> would damn the whole human race because of one momentary lapse? [Such a god would be more] like Big Brother in George Orwell's *Nineteen Eighty-four*, spying on

everything I did, thought and felt, endlessly dissatisfied, and doling out favours and punishments indiscriminately...
(*The Spiral Staircase, pp.* 234-5)

Religious Incentives to Morality

Traditionally, of course, the prospects of Heaven or Hell after death have been among the principle 'favours and punishments' offered by the Christian Church and Islam. In earlier times the existence of such 'places' is fully understandable. It was known that fire spewed out of the earth below us from volcanoes; and above us the light from the stars and the sun suggested possibilities of brightness and hope beyond our earthly domain. Why should there not be an eternal Paradise somewhere for the just? And why not an undesirable alternative for the wicked? However, the growth of scientific understanding of molecular physics, the cosmos and evolution has inevitably changed our attitudes to time, place and space. And our understanding of the nature of poetry and literary devices puts Heaven and Hell and the Garden of Eden in the same category as utopias and dystopias – Lilliput, Shangri La, Arcady, Erehwon and El Dorado. All of these are conceptual creations pointing to real truths of human experience but not to existing factual entities. The idea of eternal life as a reward needs somewhere, or some element, in which to take place; in the 21st century such an environment is very difficult to find.

There are many religious people nowadays who would agree with Dawkins that 'the idea of immortality... survives and spreads because it caters to wishful thinking.' I suppose many of us, when we see or read about 'man's inhumanity to man' so often in the media, have moments when we think that the tyrants and torturers responsible should have to receive some of their own medicine finally. And, looking at the situation more positively, a lot of us enjoy our lives sufficiently to wish them to continue indefinitely. For some, this is the rationale for good behaviour. But many good Christians, Jews, Muslims, Atheists and others don't behave morally because they hope for rewards or fear punishments from God, but from altruism and a desire to preserve their self-respect. They find their satisfaction and reward in *this* life simply by cooperating with their neighbours and promoting general well-being to the best of their ability.

Obedience and morality

To revert to the concept of obedience for earning heavenly prizes we have seen in two world wars how obedience to orders can lead to excesses. Sacrifice is one aspect of obedience. It can take both morally valid forms and forms that are morally suspect. The sacrifices made by those with a vocation for the caring professions and those who donate blood or kidneys, for example, or risk their lives rescuing others are morally commendable. They selflessly support and defend the 'will to live' of others. On the other hand this cannot be said of the 'sacrifices' made by *kamikaze* pilots, suicide bomb 'martyrs' and political leaders who claim to 'be making difficult decisions' when they sacrifice the lives of others for their own personal or national glory. The sacrifice of civilians as a result of 'collateral damage' – dismissed as 'stuff happens' in war by some military and political leaders – is equally repugnant.

The *Old Testament* story of Abraham's willingness to sacrifice his son Isaac is uncomfortable reading for most of us today. However, when it was written ritual sacrifices were widely current. Evidently the story was intended to illustrate the moral advance being made by the Hebrews *at the time*: the point being that Abraham *doesn't* in fact go ahead with the sacrifice. However, it does not present Abraham as a useful role model for the 21st century. Nor does the unedifying Protestant doctrine of the Atonement by divine sacrifice (described above) make much sense today. God as simply 'the Power we live by' is a much healthier concept. After all, Jesus of Nazareth regarded the Creator as 'our Father' whose loving support we could rely on. Dogmatic inventions and accretions like the Atonement concept are not a great deal of help.

Pride and morality

Before leaving the question of morality's relation to divinity it is necessary to consider the sin regarded in mediaeval times as the most deadly of the seven – that is pride, or *hubris*. It was wisely placed above wrath, envy, lust, gluttony, avarice and sloth, and is arguably a contributory element to some of the other six. We still see it at work in political, military, economic and religious rivalry, in the celebrity cult and social and cultural life generally. There is, of course, modest pride in a job well done, natural pleasure and satisfaction in an achievement. But the Greek word *hubris* signifies the 'deadly sin' of arrogant pride or presumption: in the Greek tragedies it was used for excessive pride in support or in defiance of the gods, leading to nemesis.

The terms *hubris* and *nemesis* might appropriately be applied, respectively, in relation to the 'rise' and 'fall' of the banking system at the close of 2008 or the comeuppance of acquisitive British Parliamentarians in

2009. It is certainly appropriate to describe the cause of the invasion of Iraq in 2003, ostensibly to remove a dictator but primarily to gain control of valuable oil supplies and to install 'regime change'. The ostensible reason is praiseworthy, but the oil supply was required to entrench power and the idea that one nation can simply implant a change of regime in a vastly different social and cultural environment was clearly an example of *hubris*. The hypocritical stockpiling of nuclear weapons while declaring that newcomers to the same crime have no rights to 'join the club' is another example of *hubris,* as was the arrogant appropriation of skies for American defence programmes by President George W. Bush at the beginning of the 21st century.

Hubris as 'honour'

Another area were *hubris* is still in operation is under the guise of 'honour'. In western society misguided understanding of the real nature of honour cost many lives in quarrels and duels throughout the centuries, with duels continuing up to the late nineteenth century. The play *Romeo and Juliet* is an excellent fictional example of tragedy arising from tribal rivalry based on 'honour'. Now it is making its mark in suicidal martyrdoms and so-called honour killings. In the martyrdoms there is at least an element of self-sacrifice, but the *hubris* is in the conception that the one life offered is worth (or more than worth) the numerous innocent lives destroyed and damaged by the explosion. For 'honour' killings there is not even an element of self-sacrifice: the perpetrators sacrifice their victims by murder, mutilation or enforced 'suicide'. The Taliban appear to be the worst offenders, their *hubris* fuelled by a misguided sense that they are somehow defending the 'purity' of their religion. Whether the more isolated, local or domestic 'honour killings' are based on religious or tribal motives is not clear, but the death-toll of thousands of women murdered annually does little credit to those Muslims who commit such atrocities. It is clear from the *Qur'an* that Mohammed sought to *improve* the lot of women. How do these 'honour'-seeking murderers imagine that they are being loyal to his example? Those who hurt and maim others in the name of 'honour' fail to understand that honour is a personal matter. Another person's behaviour can never impinge upon our personal honour. Tribal allegiance is no excuse: each individual member of a tribe or family is responsible for his or her own acts. No other person has the right to take ownership of these acts or to feel responsibility for them. The learning of mutual respect and reverence for the life in others is the only answer to the problem of crimes in the name of 'honour'.

In the original Greek sense *hubris* generally meant 'excessive pride in *defiance* of the gods', but we find that today it is at least equally applicable to pride purporting to show *loyalty* to the gods, or God. The Taliban way of expressing their loyalty is certainly not supporting the underlying divine element, the Power we live by, but tends to destruction rather than creativity, and is oblivious to love and caring. The problem derives from the way humans *create* our different gods and our moralities. We have the 'crusader' gods of the Taliban, of mediaeval Christianity, of George W. Bush's United States hegemony, of the pro-life doctor-killers, of *Al-Qaida*, of possessive Zionism, and (among a host of others) even of the 'Prosperity Gospel' faithful who believe 'God wants us to be rich'. (Which of us? All of us? How?) Certainly the leaders of some of these gospels do very well out of their benighted enthusiasms, but in the end they all, like their Greek forebears, lead towards *nemesis*.

The question asked at the beginning of this chapter was: How far does morality depend upon God, or a belief in God's existence? The answer appears to be that morality itself 'depends upon God'since everything depends upon the underlying Power we live by; but the shape or quality of the moral values that are created or discovered varies broadly according to where, when and by whom they are evolved.

How well or how far these values are lived out is another problem. Since we are all the products of the same Power it would appear that we need to learn to get on with each other a lot better, whichever gods we are serving. This requires tolerance.

CHAPTER NINE

Tolerance – X as 'the other' factor

Imagine the vanity of thinking your
enemy can do you more harm than your enmity.
St Augustine, d. c.605 C.E

The golden rule of conduct is mutual
toleration, seeing that we will never all think
alike and we shall see Truth in fragments
and from different angles of vision.
Mohandas Gandhi, 1869-1948

Paranoia reduces anxiety and guilt by
transferring to the other all the characteristics
which one does not want to recognize in oneself.
Sam Keen: Faces of the Enemy, 1986

Inter-religious Antagonism

However much religions may differ, they all presumably accept that every creature on earth – including every human being – is created by the same Power. It seems extraordinary in the circumstances that so many faithful, while extolling their Creator's benevolence, believe it is their duty to hate, humiliate or destroy fellow humans whose upbringing is not identical with their own.

We have only to log on to the Internet to see the extent of inter-religious hatred. There are well over 10,000 "hate" sites on the web. One British-based filtering company for example, Surfcontrol, reported 'an increase in American religious sites advocating extremist views and a growing number of militant Islamist sites' among others. Some of the hostility was between Christians and non-Christians, some promoted the idea of Jewish conspiracies, others offered revisionist versions of the September 11 terrorist attacks, and so on.

Newspapers and television likewise give us daily reports of religious intolerance, hatred and cruelty. After the 9/11 terrorist attacks in the USA, Muslims there and in Europe were reported to be targeted by bigoted Christian groups. On the other hand, when a white teacher in Sudan let her class choose the name Muhammad for a teddy bear 'an innocent classroom gesture was...hijacked by Muslim extremists to threats of floggings and demands of shooting after Friday prayers in Khartoum.' Palestinian Muslims in Gaza are continually harassed by their Zionist neighbours and it's still not unusual in Europe for a Jewish cemetery to be desecrated by overzealous 'Christians' or 'Islamists'. On one widely reported occasion in England a Sikh boy's hair was cut off in a racist attack by white teenagers. Racial and religious prejudices are frequently confounded in these events. In both cases 'fear of the other' is at issue: *in-group* comradeship on one side harbours *out-group* hostility to the alien challenge. In the circumstances Dawkins' observation is scarcely surprising:

Even if religion did no other harm in itself, its wanton and carefully nurtured divisiveness – its deliberate and cultivated pandering to humanity's natural tendency to favour in-groups and shun out-groups – would be enough to make it a significant force for evil in the world. (*The God Delusion*, p.262)

Dawkins gives an early example of this danger, quoting the renowned twelfth-century rabbi Moses Marmonides' commentary on the application of the sixth Commandment. "Thou shalt not kill", Marmonides explained, refers to the wilful slaying of an Israelite and the offender must be punished by the sword. 'Needless to say,' he adds, 'one is not put to death if he kills a heathen.' Here 'heathen' means 'a person of no religion' or 'someone of a different religion', therefore it seems 'someone beyond the pale'. This last expression is illuminating. The 'pale' refers to the posts that fence off an enclosed area beyond which the behaviour of those living there is unacceptable.

'Infidel' has a similar meaning to 'heathen'. Ayatollah Khomeini used the word not so long ago in the following example. Addressing the faithful on the anniversary of the Prophet Mohammed's birthday (December 12, 1983) during the Iran-Iraq War he observed that:

If one permits an infidel to continue in his role as a corrupter of the earth, his moral suffering will be all the worse. If one kills the infidel, and thus stops him from perpetrating his misdeeds, his death will be a blessing to him. For if he remains alive, he will become more and more corrupt. This is a surgical operation commanded by God the all-powerful... Thanks to God, our young people are now, to the limits of their means, putting God's commandments into action. They know that to kill the unbelievers is one of man's greatest missions.

(Quoted in Sam Keen: *Faces of the Enemy*)

This example is between different sects (Shiite and Sunni) of the *same* religion. One hopes that the 'infidel'sunnis appreciated the 'blessing' conferred on them by the Ayatollah.

Similarly, among Christians there are congregations certain that their sect alone will enjoy the anticipated 'Rapture' of relocating to Heaven while less enlightened Christians will have to make do with Hell. These communities can occur as sub-groups within all the main denominations from Roman Catholic and Anglican to various evangelical sects. An Ipsos poll in 2005 found that 79% of Americans believe in a Second Coming of Jesus and 25% of adults in the USA believed it was at least 'somewhat likely'that Jesus Christ would return to Earth 'in the coming year'. Among evangelical Christian adults 46% believed that the Coming was imminent. A web site, *End Times Bible Prophesy Made Plain*, offers advice to Christians about how to cope with the Apocalypse when it happens. It has a helpful section for the over-hopeful entitled: 'Why Most Christians Won't be Raptured (and How to Make Sure You Are.)'. Among a mass of other advice and information it offers: 'Six Wrong Ways to face the End-Times (and One Right)';'the Mark of the Beast and How to Avoid it Today'; and 'God's 6000 Year Plan: Dating Jesus' Return?' In return for all this advice you are invited to make a donation. There is no compulsion for this, but in view of what you learn from the site you might feel it worthwhile to be on the safe side and earn some credit while you can. The *Wikipedia Free Encyclopaedia* web-site gives good coverage to Apocalypse theories many of which juggle skillfully with the order and timing of the elements involved which include: the Rapture, the Tribulation, the Second Coming, the Millennium, the Last Judgement and Eternity.

A problem arising from these eschatological theories is that they tend to be coupled with the anticipation of Armageddon – the last battle between good and evil before the day of judgement. Politically this would involve a final universal battle of saints and sinners – and drag in many of us who don't feel we really belong to either category. The danger is that the eagerness of these sects to attain their 'Rapture' could, if they happen to have any political clout, promote a self-fulfilling prophecy engulfing us all. The story of the Good Samaritan is clearly lost on these disciples.

What we see all too often – within religions, between religions, and between religious, agnostics and atheists – is the expression of *in-group solidarity* and *out-group antagonism*. Every religion naturally develops in its own way, with its unique history, narrative and myths, its particular rituals, its distinctive doctrines, laws and institutions, its special buildings and sacred objects, and its distinctive appeals to the emotions. But every single member of these diverse congregations is launched into the world by the same unique Power that we live by. If we could only remember that *we are all in the same in-group* a great deal of unhappiness and bloodshed could be spared. However much our religions and philosophies may differ, we are all essentially of the same stock – our basic gene-structure is the universal proof of our kindred.

Paranoia and Projection

If there are enemies to be feared they are not so much the ones outside us as those *within* us. The worst of our enemies is probably our own capacity for enmity, frequently achieved by a psychological process called 'projection'. We owe our understanding of this phenomenon to Carl Jung who identified the concept of the *shadow* hidden in our unconscious minds. It seems that as our moral consciousness develops a split tends to evolve in our minds between the 'good', civilized desires and emotions that we relate to and strive for, and 'bad' features – such as greed, cruelty, untruthfulness and hostility, – of which (when we indulge them) we are ashamed. When we reject these negative aspects of ourselves they tend to congregate and lodge as a 'shadow' in our unconscious minds.

Unfortunately there is a common human tendency, particularly when under stress, to *project* these hidden features onto a perceived 'enemy'. We see ourselves as the 'good guys', righteous and pure, while the 'enemy' – witches, neighbours, societies or races – become the 'bad guys' saddled with our projected shadow. Paranoia, a tendency to delusions of persecution and self-importance, which exaggerates our suspicion and mistrust of others, is the result of our hidden 'shadow'. Because we live in communities, continually influencing (and sometimes contaminating) each other with our thoughts and ideas there can be group shadows as well as private shadows. It seems to be the case that authoritarian dogma-ridden or ideology-ridden societies find and define their collective shadow in terms of what is collectively repressed. During the Cold War, for example, Communist Russia saw westerners as 'decadent bourgeois capitalists' and the West (particularly in the era dominated by Senator McCarthy) tended to fear 'reds under the beds' everywhere. Arthur Miller's Play, *The Crucible*, illustrates how the community in Seventeenth century Salem objectified its collective shadow in witchcraft and hounded innocent women under this misapprehension. More recently we have had 'the War against Terror' versus what could be characterized as a 'War against Western *hubris* and hypocrisy'. It seems that the psychological feature 'projection' is probably the worst enemy that stands in the way of tolerance.

Humankind has quite enough problems on its plate just now with global warming, desertification, deforestation, tsunamis, earthquakes, starvation, mass migration, economic meltdown and so on. There has never been a time so demanding of our global cooperation as the challenging twenty-first Century. We haven't the time to waste our energies on internecine squabbling and name-calling. We have responsibilities to our maker, to each other and to the preservation of our environmental resources.

The Concept of divine favouritism

The concept of 'election' for the salvation of certain individuals or tribes presents humanity with serious problems. What kind of Creator does this presuppose? The idea of 'creative favouritism' is realistically a non-starter. All life on earth comes from the same source and is nourished by the same Power – humankind, birds, beasts, fish, insects – even germs! We might well ask if there is even a chosen *species,* let alone sect, tribe or state.

It is high time to adopt a mature approach to our global situation. We need to adjust our attitudes to the whole environment, way beyond inter-doctrinal, inter-state or inter-racial conflict. Linked with the idea of divine 'election'to a special status in the cosmic scheme is a spurious sense of unshakeable certainty felt by some believers. I recently heard on a television faith-and-science programme someone declare, 'Of course, I want Islam to take over the world – and it will!' This dangerous kind of utterance is akin to the 19th-century concept of 'the white man's burden' which for many westerners was coupled with a certainty that Christianity would eventually take over the world. Or of George W. Bush's illusion about 'regime change' – his apparent certainty that you could plant western style democracy anywhere in the world and it would take root automatically.

There is no doubt that circumstances have favoured states and communities miraculously from time to time, changing the course of history. The Jewish experience of crossing the Red Sea was one; Mohammed's encounter with a spider in a moment of despair was another; and Adolf Hitler's decision in World War Two to invade Russia instead of England another. But these extraordinary and world-changing happenings should not be construed as divine favouritism. Most of us, at some moments in our lives, have experienced extraordinary, unexpected events that have given us a needed lift out of trouble or even changed the course of our lives – but this doesn't prove that we are saints. When such timely coincidences take place for individuals, tribes or nations it's unwise to assume it's because of divine favouritism.

Challenges to security and belief

All religious individuals, agnostics or atheists who are genuinely in search of the essential foundation *underlying* their faith or outlook deserve our respect. It is obvious, given the multiplicity of religions and ideologies extant that there must be some aspects of each faith that are less certain than others. Reason dictates that each religion must have its strengths and weaknesses. In consequence we can all benefit from a degree of open-mindedness and a readiness to respect and learn from other faiths, even though we cannot agree with them in detail. What element can we find that links all, or most, religious beliefs?

Gandhi expressed his belief that love, or compassion, is the underlying element in all the major faiths when he said, 'It is the rule of love that rules humankind. Had violence, i.e. hatred, ruled us, we should have become extinct long ago.' He deeply regretted the tragic way in which 'the so-called civilized mind and nations conduct themselves as if the basis of society was violence.'

Frequently the violent word precedes the violent act. Schoolteachers know only too well how hurtful even name-calling can be. Words such as 'coward', 'fatty', 'nigger' or 'Paki', can soon start a playground fight. Generally speaking a playground fight can be quickly settled without injury. Among adults, particularly in groups, derogatory verbal insults can easily escalate to dangerous levels. Whether the terms refer to personal characteristics, racial origin or religious persuasion, the hurt is generally deeply felt. In a social situation it is painful to be regarded as different from ones peers. Fortunately, there has been considerable advance in recognizing this problem.

However, both within and between religious communities, the use of profane, disrespectful or blasphemous language is another form of verbal violence directed not so much at individuals, but to the beings or objects that different communities regard as sacred. This results from, or promotes, intolerance between members of different faiths. I am not in favour of attacking so-called 'blasphemy' by legal sanctions or book burnings: tolerance of free speech is too important an element in democratic society. However, tolerance does not necessarily imply agreement – only our respect for an individual's right to self-expression. We do not have to respect what is disrespectful. We have the same right to shun, ignore or deplore profane or blasphemous expression as others have to express it.

The book-burning and the *fatwah* imposed on Salmon Rushdie's book *The Satanic Verses* were prime examples of offence being taken on the grounds of blasphemous or disrespectful language. There is no doubt that there are genuine qualities of insight in Rushdie's book – elements which, properly understood in a literary context, are thoughtful and provocative. But there are also passages that – as the violent reaction showed – it would clearly have been more tactful to have left out. It is not surprising that many Muslims were shocked and hurt by the irreverence shown to their venerated Prophet. I am all in favour of protecting the exercise of free speech, but there are times and situations when a little tact might save a lot of lives and general disruption. While we very properly have a right to say and publish what we think or feel, whether in fiction or otherwise we also have the right, and perhaps a moral duty, to think of its potential effects on the feelings of others.

We have seen a great deal of disrespect for religious sensibility in recent years. Other notable examples include the film *The Life of Brian,* offensive to many Christians; the so-called *Beckham Nativity* where 'celebrity' waxworks assumed the role of the Holy Family in the Madame Tussauds Museum in London in 2004; and a play performed in Birmingham in 2005, offensive to many Sikhs.

Offensive as such examples of disrespect can be, there is no excuse for the application of anti-blasphemy laws. They are frequently made the excuse for acts of cruelty and revenge. Such was the case of an 11-year-old Christian girl, Rimsha, charged with blasphemy by hard-line mullahs in Pakistan in 2012. In fact, when the Pakistani authorities investigated the affair, it turned out that the charge of desecrating the *Qur'an* was unjustified. The previous year a leading politician from the ruling Pakistan Peoples party, Salman Taseer, was gunned down by one of his bodyguards after he described the statute on blasphemy as a "black law" and called for the release of a Christian woman, Asia Bibi, convicted under it.(*Guardian Weekly*, 31/8/12)

In the same news report, Saeed Shah observes that:

It is dangerous in Pakistan even to discuss blasphemy, which carries the death penalty. The law is frequently used to level false allegations in order to settle scores, with lurid tales of burning or desecrating the *Qur'an* levelled against religious minorities and fellow Muslims.

Up to the 17th century, it must be admitted, some savage punishments were given for blasphemy in England. Gradually, however, the right to free speech and the recognition that there is nothing to be gained by ruthless crushing of personal opinion has gained ground and the United Kingdom blasphemy laws were abolished in 2008. Regrettably, 45 countries in Europe still have anti-blasphemy laws of various degrees of severity.

It is obvious that no words can hurt the 'power we live by'. Such a notion belongs to an anthropomorphic conceptualisation more appropriate to the tribal gods of the past. The all-embracing 'God' that underlies all religions is 'above' and beyond the reach of verbal criticism. At the same time, deliberate mockery of what is sacred to many fellow humans suggests a lack of tact, forbearance and respect for others, often revealing intolerance.

Culture clash accelerated by global 'shrinkage'

Ever since human speech enabled humans to have ideas and opinions regarding material and spiritual matters there have no doubt been differences of view between rival exponents of religious ideas. Early scriptures describe some of the violent struggles between hostile faiths. But in the past, geography and slow communication facilitated to some extent the containment of relatively isolated homogeneous communities. In today's 'global village' clashing cultures are daily thrown together in what has been described as 'a moral and material maze'. Our problem is to find ways of reconciling different faiths and none within and between our modern, pluralistic societies. Thoughtful members of the major religions recognise that they can no longer claim to be the possessors of 'exclusive truth'. A *view* of the truth, yes, but not 'the whole truth and nothing but the truth' demanded of jurors. They recognise that though we may not be able to achieve consensus, there must at least be some element of compromise if we are to live together peacefully and fruitfully. Gandhi recognised that the ultimate truth about the mystery we call 'God' is beyond the reach of the limited human mind. Perhaps a universal religion is beyond our reach? 'Imperfect men put it into such language as they can command, and their words are interpreted by other men equally imperfect...' he said. Who can say who is right and who is wrong? Maybe everybody is wrong? 'Hence the necessity for tolerance, which does not mean indifference to one's own faith, but a more intelligent and purer love for it.' Gandhi's beliefs were also exemplified in his behaviour. He sought to understand and benefit from Islam, Christianity, Buddhism, Jainism and other faiths, but he incorporated the insights he gained from them into his Hinduism, which remained his lifelong religious base.

For Deepak Chopra, as for Gandhi, tolerance is not simply passive, but an active engagement with different faiths. In his book *How to Know God*, he recognizes the shared underlying spiritual elements in all religions. 'Awakening is at the root of the world's religions,' he writes. 'It unites prophets, messiahs, and saints into a privileged elite.' He relates the traditional accounts of the miraculous inspirations experienced in turn by Siddhartha (later the Buddha), Jesus and Muhammad. Although these stories were recorded well after they are said to have occurred 'these legends are now articles of faith' to believers, and so are entitled to our respect. Whether we believe them in detail or not is unimportant. 'The essential point is that our minds can open to the sudden inrush of light'that inspired their missions.' (pp.202-30)

The Catholic scholar Hans Kung, in *What I Believe*, advocates 'better mutual understanding and a deeper solidarity of the three faith communities' – Christians, Jews and Muslims. 'Each of the three cannot in fact really understand its nature and history without a look at the two others. How can they still regard one another as 'unbelievers' (the Christian attitude towards Jews and Muslims), or as 'apostates' (the Jewish attitude to Christians and Muslims), or as 'superseded' (the Muslim attitude to Jews and Christians)?' (p.111). Hans Kung's concern for inter-religious understanding goes well beyond the three monotheistic 'religions of the Book'. He and the Dalai Lama were two of the leading lights of the 1993 Parliament of the World's Religions that produced the excellent mission statement *Towards a Global Ethic* – an 'interfaith declaration... of the results of a two-year consultation among more than two hundred scholars and theologians representing the world's communities of faith.'since then gatherings of the Parliament of the World's Religions have taken place in Chicago (1993), Cape Town (1999), Barcelona (2004) and Melbourne (2009) with attendances ranging from 6000 to nearly 9000.

Rabbi, philosopher and theologian, Jonathan Sacks, in his book *The Dignity of Difference* applauds the bringing together of those of many different persuasions. He believes that, despite the continual violence and conflict in the world, it is our responsibility to hope. 'We are not wrong to dream, wish and work for a better world,' he writes. In our contemporary highly interconnected world:

172

We have come face to face with the stranger, and it makes all the difference whether we find this threatening or enlarging. Every scriptural canon has within it texts which, read literally, can be taken to endorse narrow particularism, suspicion of strangers, and intolerance toward those who believe differently than we do. Each also has within it sources that emphasize kinship with the stranger, empathy with the outsider, the courage that leads people to extend a hand across boundaries of estrangement or hostility. (p.207)

Whether we opt for retrenchment or outreach, 'The choice is ours,' he concludes.

Not everyone has time to attend world conferences, to write books, or to study other religions in detail, but we can all make an imaginative attempt to put ourselves in the position of someone born into another faith and try to see how they view what may seem strange to us. At the same time we cannot assume that others should automatically understand the peculiarities of our own faiths.

David Goldberg, of the Liberal Jewish Synagogue put the situation well in a letter to *The Times*:

Do not all religions in the modern world have to argue their case in the marketplace of ideas, rather than silence opponents with violent threats? To insist that everything written in the Bible or the Koran must be true for all time is not the way for religion to engage in a constructive dialogue with secular society. Agreeing on some ground rules for how we read and interpret our sacred scriptures is probably the most crucial task facing Judaism, Christianity and Islam today if we wish to foster understanding between those of all religions and none. (*The Times*, January 2006)

This recognizes the fact that time changes both the context and our understanding of our respective religions or philosophies; that there are different ways of interpreting religious language and ideas; and that it is important for us seek mutual understanding in a secular society.

Distinguishing spirituality and religion

It is important to distinguish between spirituality and religion. Spirituality is something that is shared in varying degrees by all of us. It belongs to that part of our mind (or some would say soul) not concerned with material things, but with feelings and sensitivity. Religion generally implies belief about the nature of 'God', rules, shared membership, obedience and worship. Our spirit is our *individual* response to life and, for many, to life's sacredness, while religion involves *corporate* spirituality or activity. For this reason it is generally easier to meet those of different persuasions on a spiritual level than in terms of detailed dogmatic beliefs or ritual procedures.

Many individuals, regardless of their own faith, recognize an aspect of godliness in other humans of different persuasions. An essential tenet of Christian Quakers, for example, is that 'there is that of God in every person'. In Islam the closeness of God to all human beings is arrestingly expressed in the *Qu'ran* by the image that 'Allah is nearer to man than the vein in his neck' (Chapter 50:16). No doubt we all have moments when we are touched by something 'sacred' in others. Some would call this special quality 'godliness' others would call it 'humanity'. A 'humane' act is one showing benevolence and compassion, the aim (we would hope) of both believers and non-believers.

Seeing others in sensitive ways is clearly important. It is perhaps equally important to take the poet Robert Burns' advice and try to look at ourselves objectively.

> O would some Power the giftie gie us
> To see ourselves as others see us!
> It would frae many a blunder free us.

(I have anglicized his lines somewhat.) The fact that this extract comes from a poem entitled and addressed *To a Louse* reminds us that we are *all* bound – great and small – to play our parts in the ecological network of Creation. It is useful sometimes to encounter a poem that reduces our ego and cuts us down to size.

In arguing for toleration, I have stressed the dangers of 'absolute certainty'that our own particular views or dogmas are right. This suggestion of moral and religious relativism may imply a belief that there are no certainties. This is not my intention. There is somewhere a bedrock of Truth, of material and spiritual facts that are incontestable. Perhaps your or my convictions approximate to that foundation of fundamental realities. I hope so. The danger is to *assume* that ours is the only light and to judge all others by it. We need to leave a margin in which to acknowledge, and try to understand, the sincere beliefs of others.

However, while moral and religious relativism have their place, the margin of tolerance we allow must also be subject to relativism. There is no excuse for tolerating the intolerable where dishonesty, cruelty and suffering are concerned. Finally we are judged by our actions rather than by our beliefs. Whatever our background, each person has to fall back on his or her conscience when making decisions. Toleration of others' beliefs helps us to widen our judgment. Little by little by a natural process of comparisons and contrasts we can hope to refine our individual sense of right and wrong.

Marcus Aurelius, probably the most sensitive and thoughtful of the Roman Emperors, was also a man of action: 'Let your one delight and refreshment be to pass from one service to the community to another, with God ever in mind,' he wrote in his notebook. Elsewhere, he shows that 'the community' in question was not just an 'in group':

> In what I do, I am to do it with reference to the service of mankind. In what befalls me, I am to accept it with reference to the gods, and to that universal source from which the whole close-linked chain of circumstance has its issue. (p.125)

Marcus Aurelius lived in a world which was doubtless even more divided by tribalism than ours is. However, the dangers of in-group cooperation and out-group hostility did not then pose a global threat as they do today.

Four centuries after the death of Marcus Aurelius, and a century after the Romans no longer occupied Britain, the Anglo-Saxon King, Ethelbert, was reigning over the steadily cohering tribes in the southern counties of early England. In 597 he welcomed the arrival of a Roman visitor, Augustine, who proposed to introduce Christianity to 'England'. Ethelbert's tactful speech is instructive as a lesson in toleration:

Your words are fair, and your promises – but because they are new and doubtful, I cannot give my assent to them, and leave the customs which I have so long observed, with the whole Anglo-Saxon race. But because you have come hither as strangers from a long distance, and as I...have seen clearly that what you yourselves believed to be true and good, you wish to impart to us, we do not wish to molest you; nay, rather we are anxious to receive you hospitably, and to give you all that is needed for your support, nor do we hinder you from joining all whom you can to the faith of your religion.
(From Stanley's *Memorials of Canterbury*, v. Ernest Rhys, 1915)

If we could all adopt such an open-minded and tolerant spirit the world might be a safer place. Tolerance is not always easy to acquire and has to be worked on. Likewise, open-mindedness is not empty-mindedness: it implies the achievement of a state of provisional certainty combined with confidence that encounters with new or contrary truths are not necessarily threatening.

In a world threatened by climate change, the persistence of inter-cultural hostility, and the possibility of nuclear annihilation many of us may have to make adjustments to our beliefs and attitudes. The next chapter suggests ways in which such modifications might be achieved.

CHAPTER TEN

The X-Factor and intelligent religion

We should take care not to make the intellect our god; it has, of course, powerful muscles, but no personality.
Albert Einstein: Out of My Later Years, 1950

My dear child, you must believe in God despite of what the clergy tell you.
Benjamin Jowett (V-C. of Oxford University) on his deathbed, 1893

The golden rule is to test everything in the light of reason and experience, no matter from where it comes.
Mahatma Gandhi, 1869-1948

What is intelligent religion?
By 'intelligent religion' I mean religion that makes sense today. A computer has a kind of intelligence, but it is bound by strict, predetermined, instructions; its programmed responses are automatic and inflexible, and cannot adapt

readily to change. Moreover, its knowledge is finitely limited to the material that has been previously loaded into it. (If this sounds suspiciously like fundamentalism, so be it.) There are, apparently, some machines that are *'able to vary their behaviour in response to varying situations and requirements and past experience'*. This certainly doesn't describe my laptop; but, if they exist, such machines function pretty much like an intelligent human. That is also how 'intelligent religion'should function. A.D 2000 is very different from 2000 B.C., or even from A.D. 600 when the 'final' prophet of the 'three revealed religions' was operating. Our thinking and behaviour today has to take account of these differences when it uses texts written in ancient times.

There have been, and are, probably as many ways of imagining 'God' as there are individual human beings. Each one of us constructs his or her image and understanding from their own background, talking, reading and experience of life. There are clearly different ways of serving, worshipping or rejecting the divine. However, people are initially constrained by their circumstances and upbringing to belong to a particular religious or other grouping. Later, if they have a free choice, they congregate with a body that most closely resembles their particular construction. So one is, or becomes, a Christian, Moslem, Jew, Buddhist, Jain, Hindu, Agnostic, Atheist, or Humanist. Each of these (and most other) religions or ideologies claims to favour peace and harmonious living. How is it that with all this apparent goodwill our world is in such a mess?

In just one newspaper (*Guardian Weekly, 10/16 July 2009)* I find reports of large-scale hunger resulting from man-made climate change; deforestation of the Amazon jungle by mining; 'acquisition of farmland from the poor by rich countries'; disastrous flooding in Zambia; nuclear proliferation (both for power and military purposes); dangerous population growth; massive displacement of populations due to wars and economic mismanagement; poverty and unemployment due to financial risk-taking and banking meltdown.

At the same time as all this is happening there are 'religiously'-motivated suicide bombings in different parts of the world; there is a quasi-Christian drug cartel, 'La Familia', operating in Mexico; religious strife in Pakistan, Iran, Iraq, Israel, Palestine and Afghanistan; ideological strife in Burma, China and North Korea; the 'abduction and beheading of a journalist who had made remarks perceived to be insulting towards Islam'; friction in the Anglican Christian community regarding the ordination of women and gay priests, and more...

There is an extraordinary lack of any sense of proportion in the way our energies are applied. Our real enemies are climate change, inequality and selfishness, and the plundering of our natural environment; yet we are embattled about women priests, sexual orientation and 'perceived insults'. Obviously not all the problems we face have a religious origin. But since religions claim to be so concerned about our world and our relationships they should at least be concentrating their efforts towards being part of the solution. This is what I mean by 'intelligent religion': making a concerted effort to get below the surface differences between one faith and another and to work with the universal Power we live by in an attempt to bring about some of the changes we must all presumably desire.

Religion and science

The quest for Truth is claimed by both the religious faithful and the atheistic humanist. Since there is such a vast range of opinion in the world, we all know that our own success in this quest must be problematic and partial. However, there is a level of understanding where all men and women of goodwill can meet: there is no essential quarrel between science and religion. By different routes St Francis of Assisi and Charles Darwin, seven centuries later, came to virtually the same conclusion. St. Francis recognised animals and birds as his 'brothers and sisters'. Later, after years of arduous scientific research, Darwin seems to have proved conclusively that we are all related. Environmental and genetic studies are confirming their insights for us all.

Judaic, Christian and Islamic cultures have all produced creative scientists, philosophers, mathematicians and sociologists. In *Living Islam,* Akbar Ahmed reminds us that *ilm,* knowledge, is emphasized throughout the *Qur'an.* According to Mohammed, 'The first thing created by God was the Intellect.' Christianity has come a long way since St Augustine denounced the 'disease of curiosity' and warned against its danger, declaring: 'It is this which drives us to try and discover the secrets of nature, those secrets which are beyond our understanding, which can avail us nothing and which man should not wish to learn.' The Inquisition that persecuted Galileo and other so-called 'heretics' fortunately belongs to the past, and Christianity has generally embraced the beneficial developments in science, technology and medicine that we now enjoy.

In light of former achievements of Islam in mathematics, science and medicine, it is distressing to read of the behaviour of deviant Islamists today attacking education.

The Guardian Weekly (19.07.13) reports how Abubaker Shekau, the leader of Nigeria's Islamist militant group Boko Haram, encourages his followers to target schools 'until our last breath'. He sees western education as a 'plot against Islam' and swears: 'Teachers who teach western education? We will kill them in front of their students, and tell the students to henceforth study the Qur'an.' The result: in the last four years, 'more than 300 classrooms have been torched in the remote, arid state [of north-eastern Yobe in Nigeria] according to official counts.'

An article in the same issue of *The Guardian Weekly* tells of a 16-year-old girl, Malala Youafzai, shot in the head by a Pakistani Taliban fanatic for supporting the education of girls. After nine months of surgical interventions she is addressing an assembly in the United Nations:

I am not against anyone, (she says). Neither am I here to speak in terms of personal revenge against the Taliban...The extremists are afraid of books and pens. The power of education frightens them. They are afraid of women. The power of the voice of women frightens them... that's why they are blasting schools every day – because they are afraid of change...

They think that God is a tiny little conservative being who would send girls to hell just because of going to school. The terrorists are misusing the name of Islam and Pashtun society for their own personal benefits. Islam is a religion of peace, humanity and brotherhood. Islam says that it is not only each child's right to get education, rather it is their duty and responsibility.

These two reports give us, in stark contrast, the voice of modern forward-looking Islam against that of the negative and retrogressive Islamists.

In a BBC broadcast (*Thought for the Day*, 1 February, 2007), a Sikh scholar, Dr Jeevan Singh Deol, suggested that both within and between religions in Britain we urgently need 'some fresh thinking on what it means in the here and now to be a Sikh, a Muslim, a Jew or a Christian.' He argued that 'this will mean having to question, and sometimes even to challenge, our inheritances as faith communities – and not just at the level of rules and codes of conduct.' This is sound advice, appropriate not just for Britain alone, but worldwide. It is interesting that Dr Deol believes faith leaders need to look 'more *deeply*' [my italics] into the resources of their religions'. By this means they may 'start to come to grips not just with the relationship between religions but also with the connection between the lives of believers and those of society as a whole.' There is no suggestion here that one's religion is weakened by contact with other ways of thought, but rather the implication that it can be strengthened.

Another scholar who urges that we seek to recognize the values in different religions is Karen Armstrong. She found that this helped her in the assessment, understanding and enrichment of her own faith. With no detriment to the continued pursuit of 'that longing for the sacred', she found herself 'beginning to think differently, and to realise that assumptions that had hitherto held [her] in thrall were by no means cast in stone.' Her new freedom of thought led her to the conclusion that there was an underlying unity in the universal, but multi-faceted, search for God, and that 'the one and only test of a valid religious idea, doctrinal statement, spiritual experience or devotional practice was that it must lead directly to practical compassion.' Her studies convinced her that the true religious quest is 'not to latch on to some superhuman personality or to get to heaven, but to discover how to be fully human.' Iconic figures such as Muhammed, the Buddha and Jesus show us that 'men and women have a potential for the divine, and are not complete unless they realize it within themselves.' The 'divine' then for Karen Armstrong is both practical (in the here and now) and sacred. It is something beyond us that we 'long for' and yet within us (at our best). It is both transcendent and immanent.

A shared sense of wonder

There are levels where the concerned atheist and the devout faith-holder come very close. The power we live by – X – is shared universally. Our altruism stems from our awareness of that shared understanding whether or not we belong to the devout.

Dawkins, despite his objections to organized religions, is not only clearly concerned with human morality, but at times expresses a sense of wonder almost corresponding (in religious terms) to a sense of the *numinous*. Take, for example, his feeling about creation as expressed in *The God Delusion*:

On one planet, and possibly only one planet in the entire universe, molecules that would normally make nothing more complicated than a chunk of rock, gather themselves together into chunks of rock-sized matter of such staggering complexity that they are capable of running, jumping, swimming, flying, seeing, hearing, capturing and eating other such animated chunks of complexity; capable in some cases of thinking and feeling, and falling in love with yet other chunks of complex matter...'

The word 'miracle' has two definitions in *The Oxford English Reference Dictionary*: (1) 'an extraordinary event attributed to some supernatural agency' and (2) 'any remarkable occurrence... [or]... a remarkable development in some specified area'. In the second sense, Dawkins clearly regards creation as a miracle. It is just that he sees it as a 'natural' miracle rather than a 'supernatural' one. We shouldn't be put off by the repeated word 'chunks': however religious we are we can't deny that we are made of chunks of matter. Dawkins shares with many of us – pious, agnostic or atheist – a sense of the 'miracle'that we can run about, think, feel and even fall in love.

Charles Darwin's conclusion to *The Origin of Species* similarly reveals a spiritual sense of wonder at the 'grandeur' of the evolutionary process,

with its several powers having been originally breathed into a few forms or into one: and that, while this planet has gone cycling on, according to the fixed law of gravity, from so simple a beginning, endless forms, most beautiful and most wonderful, have been and are being evolved.

As scientists, Dawkins refers to 'molecules' and 'chunks of matter' and Darwin to 'the law of gravity', but this in no way diminishes their sense of wonder at the creative process – which is the Power we live by.

It is difficult to understand the thinking of those Christians who seek to promote so-called 'Creationism' or

'Intelligent Design' as a *scientific* alternative to the theory of evolution in schools. Poetry and science are both valid in their own right, but it is unfair to try to teach children that they are the same thing. In America, it seems, many children's minds are being muddled in this way. Fortunately, Britain's leading scientific academy, the Royal Society, has issued a statement expressing its concern about the practice before it takes root in the United Kingdom, affirming that 'young people are poorly served by deliberate attempts to withhold, distort or misrepresent scientific knowledge...to promote particular religious beliefs' (*Guardian Weekly, 21-7-06)*. This statement is not an attack on religion, but an objection to the deliberate distortion of well-established scientific knowledge by certain misguided groups.

Evolution is still called a theory, but the continual weight of reinforcement by archaeological, physical and genetic discovery qualify it now to be regarded, for the foreseeable future at least, as reasonably established fact. The creation story told in Genesis was never intended to be understood even as a theory, let alone as a fact. It was one of many ancient creation poems about the origin of the cosmos, man's place in the world and our relationship with the Power that sustains us. Every ancient society – from the African, European and Asian continents to the Pacific Islands – had its poetic creation stories. The ancient myths, of course, still have poetic value – so long as we understand them as symbolic.

Strangely enough, the fundamentalists who believe the ancient Creation poem to be factual history are glad to use television, the Internet and other products of scientific advance in their efforts to persuade others to share their outdated notion. They seem to be quite happy to dwell in a kind of schizophrenic no-man's-land, suspended between ancient myth and modern machinery. They don't appear to be able to appreciate that our capacity for spirituality is a constant no matter how far the *Zeitgeist* shifts.

Growing Recognition of Shared Spirituality

Fortunately there are movements endeavouring to counter the schizophrenic worldview of such fundamentalists. In the words of Diana Schumacher,

> We need to reconnect the spiritual universe with daily reality and what we do in our everyday lives and to the environment. By this, I mean demonstrating transcendent spiritual values in the field of economics, social and environmental justice and, above all, in education, in our working lives, and in the search for peace at all levels. There are, thankfully many signs that this is happening, nurtured by small groups and committed spiritual people around the globe and from many different faiths and cultures.
>
> (*The Gandhi Way*, No.94 Winter 2007, p.12)

Diana Schumacher is careful to point out that 'spirituality' is not to be confused with 'religion' which is 'an institutionalized set of collectively shared beliefs and practices that vary from culture to culture'. However, she acknowledges as an important feature of all the main religious traditions that 'they all perceive spirituality as a personal condition. They refer to a spiritual person rather than a spiritual collectivity.' However, this inwardness is widely shared. 'But while I believe that spirituality is personal in its incarnation,' she continues, 'its presence is global and universal.' Diana Schumacher also quotes the definition of spirituality offered by the Budapest Business Centre's 10-year Report (2007). It is 'a search for meaning that transcends material well-being and focuses on basic deep-rooted human values and a relationship with a universal source, power or divinity.' In other words spirituality is a way of acknowledging and relating to 'X' – the Power we live by.

In a similar spirit to that of the Budapest Business Centre, Satish Kumar, editor of *Resurgence,* insists that 'reverence for nature needs to be at the heart of the world's political and social debate'to counteract the insistent mantra of "realism".

Kumar argues that 'the spiritual aspect of the environment has been lost in the great debate about the way we live, and that the broad environment movement has not understood the power of concepts such as love and reverence, which are not to be confused with religion... People look at nature from a utilitarian point of view, see what is good for them only...and seek to manage it rather than to protect it.' (*Guardian Weekly, 7.3.08).* I take it by this that the writer has in mind such issues as the mass production of meat. There is certainly no spirituality or reverence for nature in the mass marketing of battery chickens and the unnatural rearing of pigs in confined cages to make cheap meat; or the cruel force-feeding of geese to make expensive *foie gras.* The only issue at stake for the faceless multinational enterprises in the global economy is the market value of a product.

Marcus Aurelius seems to have had a good grasp of spirituality, and of its relationship to God, to Nature and to intelligence:

...nothing can come about except in obedience to Nature...this is the only way in which things have always happened, will always happen and do always happen... [Remember] the closeness of man's brotherhood with his kind; a brotherhood not of blood or human seed, but of a common intelligence... [This] intelligence in every man is God, an emanation from the deity.

(*Meditations*, Penguin, 1964)

He reminds us that 'nothing is properly a man's own, for even his child, his body, his soul itself, all come from this same God'. Here 'God', 'Nature' and 'intelligence' all clearly relate to the Power we live by.

'Intelligent' nature

It seems to me that there is an awful lot of 'intelligence' in Nature – in other words, in the behaviour of matter. This is obviously not the same kind of intelligence that humans pride themselves upon – thinking, arranging ideas and (occasionally) coming to correct conclusions. The intelligence I am thinking of is even more intimate than the instinctive intelligence of an animal. Maybe 'innate' is the nearest I can get. And perhaps I should say '*knowledge*' rather than 'intelligence'. For example, the bindweed *knows* how to climb up another plant; light and sound *know* how to travel at their appropriate speeds; sperm *knows* how to combine with ova, and together they *know* how to sort out the complex genetic elements between them; oxygen has no particular trouble joining up with hydrogen to make water – they *know* the correct proportions; and so on. In fact, natural elements seem to be more reliable in their behaviour than human beings.

I had been mulling over this thought for some time when I came across an article in the *Sunday Times* (12.8.07) headed 'Dust "comes alive" in space'. Apparently scientists have encountered a situation in which 'inorganic material can assume 'the characteristics of living organisms in space', a discovery that puts a new light on the nature of alien life:

> An international panel from the Russian Academy of Sciences, the Max Planck institute in Germany and the University of Sydney found that galactic dust could form spontaneously into helixes and double helixes and that the inorganic creations had memory and the power to reproduce themselves.
>
> …The particles are held together by electromagnetic forces that the scientists say could contain a code comparable to the genetic information held in organic matter.

This seems to be a further example of a kind of 'knowledge' in matter. It doesn't worry me that part of the Power we live by may involve this kind of knowledge and the activity of electromagnetic forces. Scientific description in no way reduces the miracle of life – in fact it enhances it. I can revere the Power that brought me into the world and sustains me from day to day as sacred, because it is the highest power I know. When I wake up refreshed in the morning it is as though my batteries have been recharged overnight. Clearly I am using electrical batteries metaphorically here. But we don't have to think of matter and spirit as being always and entirely separate. It seems to me that a dictionary definition of 'spiritual' as

'...concerning the spirit *as opposed to matter'* [my italics] can be misleading. There is a way of seeing material things and processes as imbued with spirit.

The fact that 'spirituality' must not be confused with organized 'religion' does not imply that religions are without spirituality. Of course, at their best, spirituality is at the heart of religions. The trouble is that what Dawkins calls 'the baggage that the word "God" carries in the minds of most religious believers'sometimes gets in the way of the spiritual element. Dawkins ignores the potential value that exists in ritual, myth, fasting, prayer and other formal aspects of organized religion; but he is right to point out that the mechanics too often obscure the essence.

All religions are man-made

We have to remember that all religions are *'X'* + *Elaboration* (or in Dawkins' term, 'baggage'). All the elaborations being man-made, they can accordingly be modified or re-made, providing we don't lose sight of their purpose and value. We must recognise, too, that the committees and (to some extent, the prophets) who founded and developed our religions had to juggle with, create and manipulate abstract ideas and disparate facts into 'articles' and 'bodies of belief' for others.

To take a simple example, the late Roman Catholic Pope, Benedict XVI, recently reinstated the granting of 'indulgencies', releasing pilgrims going to Lourdes in 2008 from some of their time in Purgatory (the place or state of temporary suffering or expiation for ones sins). Presumably he and his cardinals had some discussion of this before the promulgation was announced. This act, in turn, raises the issue of the 'invention' of Purgatory itself. Apparently the

Council of Florence in 1439 promulgated the first decree on the subject of Purgatory. While the Roman Catholics still have Purgatory, the Church of England rejected it in 1562 by Article XXII of its Articles of Religion. We can imagine the committee work involved in all these processes. But the scholastic jockeying with the concept must leave some of the faithful suspended between heaven and earth wondering whether or not they have a place to go to expiate their sins.

The dogma of the 'Assumption' (the miraculous elevation to heaven of the body of the Virgin Mary) is another example of committee work. Although not a new idea it was not until 1950 that Pope Pius XII pronounced it an article of faith for the Roman Catholic Church – no doubt after discussing the matter with his cardinals. Apparently, the Assumption has been celebrated on August 15th since the 4th Century, but now the event is 'official'.

The concept of the Trinity was first mooted (under the term 'Triad') by Theophilus of Antioch (c. AD120). It was Tertulian who introduced the term Trinity (c. AD217). In due course it became the official doctrine of the Christian Church.

The three examples I quote – Purgatory, the Assumption and the Trinity – are taken from the Christian religious tradition, the one I am most familiar with. But the principle demonstrated can be assumed to apply to the formation and development of religious doctrines across the spectrum.

Taking the last dogma quoted – the Trinity – I find oddly enough that now I am no longer bound by the creeds and formulas that irked me before I left the Church of England for Quakerism, I can understand why the concept of the Trinity was taken up by the committees of the early

Church. The Father, the Son and the Holy Spirit – the *Creator*, *Jesus* and the psychic energy or *Spirit* that linked them – made a convenient triad persuasively yoking together power and purpose, the awesome and the ideal. Unfortunately, the schoolmen and their successors pressed their ideas too far, communicating symbolic concepts as though they were *facts,* and leaving Christianity finally burdened with beliefs such as the horrific Protestant dogma of Justification in which God cruelly sacrifices his only Son for our sins. (Some would say 'mercifully' or 'lovingly' instead of 'cruelly'. But this is not the way I see 'X', the Power we live by, functioning.)

Before leaving the subject of man-made conceptual developments in religion, it is worth pointing out that even the concept of Fundamentalism – although not a new phenomenon – was only established as a Christian movement in the USA about 1919, under the leadership of William Jennings Bryan, a politician, orator and founding editor of *The Commoner.* It quickly became popular because it saved believers from the trouble of thinking about their religion in relation to a world that had vastly changed since it was founded. More recently, Islam has suffered from a major boost of fundamentalism since the arrival of Ayatollah Khomeini in Iran and the activities of the Taliban in Afghanistan.

Meaning of 'eternal life'

One of the things dear to fundamentalists as to many other Christians, Muslims and members of other faiths is the prospect of eternal life. The concept of another life after death in this world appeals (as Freud and Dawkins point out) to our 'wishful thinking'. Eternal life seems to be preferable to death; and it is also an encouragement to virtue, especially when linked to the concept of a Day of Judgment. An Islamic leaflet on the subject deals with these issues in the following terms. 'When the idolaters of Makkah denied even the possibility of life after death, the *Qur'an* exposed the weakness of their stand by advancing very logical and rational arguments in support of it.'two of these arguments are neatly summarized later in the leaflet as follows:

> The belief in life after death not only guarantees success in the Hereafter but also makes this world full of peace and happiness by making individuals most responsible and dutiful in their activities.

The leaflet goes on to show how the immoral tribes of Arabia changed – 'as soon as they accepted the belief in the One God and life after death... They gave up their vices, helped each other in hours of need, and settled all their disputes on the basis of justice and equality.'

Give or take a little bit of poetic exaggeration in the report of this conversion, I am quite prepared to accept that a substantial improvement took place. The moral and scientific success of Islamic development is on record. However, it has to be admitted that the undisputed change in the behaviour of the 'idolaters of Makkah' was the result of their *'belief* in a fact' – or rather two facts – not of 'facts'themselves. By their very nature it is impossible to prove, or to disprove, that there is life after death or a Day of Judgement. These concepts can be asserted and believed, but they cannot be *guaranteed*.

This raises the question of means and ends. If people behave well because they fear Hell and hope for an eternity in Heaven then it seems to be a good idea to encourage them to believe these concepts to be facts. It is hard not to suspect that this is the well-meaning reasoning of the religions that promote this concept. But given our changing knowledge of the universe as a result of astronomy, microbiology, geography and scientific discovery in general, shouldn't we now recognize that these poetic concepts are intended as signposts to guide our behaviour and not as facts? Does the end justify the means? Are there not other means to encourage people to be virtuous? The Power we live by has enabled us to develop a conscience, and in this way our behaviour is *daily* subject to judgement.

It is interesting that the leaflet quoted above couples the belief in 'One God' with the belief in 'life after death'. Surely it is possible to believe in one without the other. However, this depends on *how* one conceives God. God as X – 'the Power we live by' – doubtless implies eternity, since it seems reasonable to suppose that this Power has always existed and will continue for ever. But the existence of Eternity doesn't require that we creatures have to inhabit any more of it than the brief spell on earth that we are granted. We cannot even guarantee the length of this spell, let alone what happens after it.

Religious belief and committees

Nearly every article of belief in the various religions extant has been established by a committee of some kind. It is good to see that there are signs that many sincere people of different faiths are realizing that different times might mean different rules and concepts, and are working to make necessary changes.

The Archbishop of Zambia, Emmanuel Milingo, for example, has founded a movement called 'Married Priests Now'to promote married clergy. This 'disobedient' action forced Pope Benedict XVI to lead a meeting of Church officials in Rome for '"reflection" on the subject of celibacy *(The Times, 16.11.06).* This is a vital first step in an important direction both to reduce the problems of sexual abuse due to an unnatural lifestyle and to ensure a supply of men (and maybe one day women?) to take up some of the many vacancies in the priesthood.

In the independent Arab Sheikhdom of Qatar, the First Lady, Shaika Mozah, is working to promote women's rights in terms of education and to restore the fuller participation in society she maintains women had 'in the golden age of Islam' *(Time, 16.5.08).* And in Turkey, a number of Islamic scholars are attempting a bold design 'to rewrite the basis for Islamic *sharia* law while also officially reinterpreting the *Qur'an* for the modern age' *(Guardian Weekly, 7.3.05).* They are working to create 'a twenty-first century form of Islam, fusing Muslim beliefs and traditions with European and western philosophical methods and principles' and in the process 'banishing some of the brutal penalties associated with Islamic law, such as stoning and amputation.' This is welcome news.

However, we in the west cannot afford to gloat. While we naturally condemn such cruel customs today, we must not forget that western Christianity has not all that long been cleared from similar stains.

Meaning and purpose

Working towards unity from another angle, it is encouraging to see a confirmed atheist, Terry Eagleton, taking an interest in the 'mystical'. In his book, *The Meaning of Life* (2007), he reminds us that, though modern science can tell us *how* things work 'What is mystical is not how the world is, but *that* it is.' Given this amazing fact, he says, we have to find our own meaning and purpose. The purpose should not simply be passing pleasure, which humans share with animals. Indeed it is not even an answer to a question, but rather 'a matter of living life in a certain way'. It is an ethical construct and involves 'treating others as you want them to treat you, caring for those close to you, helping strangers, and thinking long term'. (*Guardian Weekly, 29.3.07*) At the least, Terry Eagleton is advocating the Golden Rule and putting it in a long-term, cosmic setting. This is a step towards religious thinking.

Eagleton's comment on purpose is interesting. Most Christians and Muslims declare themselves concerned with God's purpose in the world. Roman Catholics tend to accept the interpretation of God's purpose offered by the reigning Pope and his Cardinals. Orthodox Protestants – if that isn't a contradiction in terms – usually look for purpose in scriptural texts. Quakers, on the other hand, endeavour to *apprehend* the divine purpose as they sit in silence in their Meeting Houses. Their search for meaning and purpose is of course based essentially on the life and teaching of Jesus but they are open to other insights wherever they seem appropriate. A Meeting of Quakers (more formally known as the Society of Friends) can be composed of members with a wide range of views and interpretations of life's 'meaning', although all will share recognition of the importance of love and of service.

It seems to me that each individual must find his or her own meaning in life, but that we can share purposes such as working in our small ways towards the advancement and survival of humankind at its best and the environment at its richest. Such purposes seem to reflect the thrust of the Power we live by. One has to be very careful in waiting on 'God's purpose' since it can all too easily turn out to be simply a reflexion of one's own. I knew a family some while ago who moved from Brixton to Tunbridge Wells because 'God told them to'. The fact that this was not long after the Brixton riots may have been incidental.

Our 'purposes' can be small-scale individual or domestic affairs, or big-scale purposes, often interpreted as 'destinies'. In the distant past the rise of the Greek and Roman Empires was achieved by notable 'heroes' who felt it their destiny to enlarge their territories, whether in order to spread their version of civilization, or simply for the love of power. They attributed their successes to numerous gods, but principally to Zeus (the Greeks) and Jupiter (the Romans). Later, in the name of Allah, inspired by the 'purpose' and destiny of Muhammad, Islam spread from the Middle East into Asia, Europe and Africa. Subsequently the nominally Christian powers of the West carved up and colonized vast areas of territory with the ostensible purpose of spreading 'the white man's burden' of Christian civilization, while conveniently in the process acquiring profitable booty to enrich their various parent countries.

We have to be careful about 'purposes' offered with religious fervour by politicians and governments. In fairly recent history we have seen how charismatic and influential men have defined 'purposes' for mankind or for sections of mankind. Napoleon designed an imperial purpose for France. Joseph Stalin's purpose after abandoning his studies for the priesthood and appropriating the humane, but godless, ideals of Karl Marx, was to create a vast imperial Communist dictatorship. Adolf Hitler's purpose was to create a Third Reich in the name of fascism, with its dogmas of racial inequality, violence and unquestioned centralised power. We have watched the rise and fall of these imperial designs, and the appalling suffering and waste of life that has accompanied them. Not surprisingly, we become suspicious of 'purposes' and recognise the importance of long term rather than short-term religious and political designs. Faced with climate change and other challenges, we are beginning to think of purposes like leaving a stable world for our grandchildren, great-grandchildren and beyond them into eternity – whatever that may bring.

Most people like to feel that their life has a 'meaning' and this quest tends to find or foster purposes so that the implications of the meaning can be fulfilled. Many people take these meanings and purposes 'off the hook', so to speak, since ready-made dogmas provide convenient points of reference, and save the trouble of thinking out one's place and possibilities in the scheme of things. Others have to wrestle with conflicting ideas and ideals in the attempt to achieve relative peace of mind.

Intelligent religion means thoughtful religion, not mechanical response to dogma but listening and thoughtful adjustment to the needs of changing times and circumstances. When trying to interpret the 'mind' of God we must remember that it is anthropomorphic thinking to speak of 'God's mind' as though it exists as a rather giant-sized version of our own. (It is even possible that humankind *is,* collectively, the mind of God. But to pursue this line of thought too far would be to get embroiled and lost in an impenetrable mystery.)

Rather than conceive of an 'external' driving mind or purpose for the world, I prefer to dwell thankfully on the wonderful phenomenon that Creation is, and on the miracle that you and I have been privileged to be introduced into it. I think of the creative Power as having 'fathered' me (or perhaps 'mothered' me), though I recognise that this again is an anthropomorphic way of thinking. When Christians speak of Jesus as 'the way, the truth and the light' I interpret this as the way Jesus responded to the 'fatherhood' of the creative Power that works through nature to promote and maintain life. And I think of Jesus of Nazareth as an exemplary man who threw light on the true way that humans should live together if they were to follow their inner conscience. When I use the prayer he taught his disciples to say – 'Our Father, who art in heaven…' – I think of the 'fathering' aspect of the Power we live by, and an imaginary, idealized vision of Creation with our part played in it at its best. That, if only it could be achieved, would be heaven.

Inter-faith enrichment

It is good news that there are now numerous inter-faith projects that bring members of different faiths into friendly contact. We are not obliged to agree with our new contacts, nor to change radically our own beliefs. But we are forced to reflect about our own beliefs in a broader context, thus discovering what is essential and what is secondary.

Whatever our own persuasion it is always instructing to take note of other interpretations. For example, even within the Judeo-Christian-Muslim monotheistic progression, Judaism rejects the Messiahship of Jesus (leaving him entirely human); Islam rejects the Trinity as an impossibility; Western Christianity rejects violent justice (as in some of the applications of sharia law in Islam) while countenancing the stocking and potential use of nuclear weapons; Judaism and Islam are ambivalent about women's role; Christianity generally favours total sexual equality; and so on. These are generalizations, but illustrate the kind of things than can spark off new thinking about one's own beliefs and prejudices.

The process of examining our particular religious or philosophical inheritance in the light of alternative worldviews can be a means of recognising the relative significance and value of the elaborations of our faith and discovering what is the true core element. In general this is likely to be a recognition that, whatever our differences, we live by a Power greater than ourselves, which is shared by all of us and finally remains a mystery.

Redefining our faiths

Perhaps each faith should locate its key element, its 'leitmotif' and check all its subsidiary aspects accordingly. For example, Christianity claims to worship a God of Love. How does that accommodate the blessing of nuclear weapons by ordained ministers or priests, past and modern crusades using violence and even allowing torture? Islam worships Allah, the Compassionate and Merciful; how can forced marriages, cruel punishments such as flogging, mutilating and stoning and 'honour killings' be accommodated in such a religion? Ultra-Orthodox Judaism puts ancient custom above contemporary accommodation. And so on. This kind of examination generally resolves itself into the question of 'means and ends'. It might be said that cruel *means* are justified by the *end* of maintaining a moral society, or promoting a great cause. But a society is only as moral as the means it uses for its ends. Nazism and Stalinist Communism proved this. Means must be regarded as ends in themselves for any just society or religion.

It may not be possible to summarise 'in a nutshell' *all* that makes for 'intelligent religion'! But if we are to solve the problems created by 'antagonistic religions' and to learn to work together to save the planet we need to consider some guiding principles. I suggest that any intelligent religion would need to recognise and incorporate the following elements in its structure:

o   the Golden Rule: 'do to others as you would have them do to you';

o   an attitude of *reverence for Life* – of fellow humans, other creatures and the natural environment;

o   promotion of cooperation for a peaceful world.

o   amendment and interpretation of the subsidiary details of the religion concerned to accord with its key theme, or core element;

o   ensuring that the Means are always appropriate to the Ends;

o   recognizing and acknowledging symbolism in abstract concepts such as destiny, heaven, hell, devil, angel, the Trinity, and others as appropriate;

o ensuring that doctrinal statements, spiritual experience or devotional practice must lead directly to practical compassion;

o finally, in our scientific age, taking note of William James' dictum that

> The God whom science recognises must be a god of universal laws exclusively. He cannot accommodate his processes to the convenience of individuals' (*The Varieties of Religious Experience, 1902*).

Perhaps we should also add the counterbalance of the last element: a recognition that the science that religion recognises may be great at describing how things work and enabling wonderful advances in technology, medicine, etc; but it is not itself a 'God'. As the old saying goes: 'Man proposes,' but ultimately God – the Power we live by – 'disposes'.

What I call intelligent religion may seem to some too earthbound, too pantheistic. If the Power we Live by is everywhere with the forces of Nature and tolerant of a range of gods, does this not make it too distant and impersonal?

I hope to show in the next chapter that, on the contrary, it makes it more personal.

CHAPTER ELEVEN

X as Personal

> *God depends on us. It is*
> *through us that God is achieved.*
> Andre Gide, Journals, 1939-50

> *Reverence the highest in yourself: it*
> *is of one piece with the Other, since in yourself*
> *also it is that to which all the rest minister,*
> *and by which your life is directed.*
> Marcus Aurelius, Meditations, 121-180 C.E.

> *The only God that is of any use is a being who is*
> *personal, supreme, and good, and whose existence*
> *is as certain as that two and two make four.*
> Somerset Maugham, The Summing Up, 1958

What do we mean by personal?

I want to show in this chapter how recognizing fully the 'X factor' – the *Power we live by*, the one unifying element in all religions and none – can transform our capacity to adapt rationally to a changing worldview and yet contribute to our *personal* spirituality and happiness.

When people speak of a 'personal God'the term can have either, or both, of two meanings: (1) a God who is himself a 'person', or (2) a God to whom we can personally relate. It should be clear by now that my conception of the Power we live by is not the first of these options However, even for those whose God is centred on a 'Person' the *Power we live by* will always be an underlying element associated with the divinity or intermediary in question – whether it be Jesus, Allah, Brahma, Shakti or another. My concentration on this underlying factor of all religions derives from my concern with our urgent, universal need to find some unifying element in all our various strivings for spiritual understanding. In any case I believe that by concentrating on the highest common factor in all religions we find a divine element with which each of us can identify closely because it is contained in, and shared by, all of us. It is intimate and universal; personal and public; immanent and transcendent.

There is no need for the faithful to abandon devotion to Jesus, Mohammed, Jehovah or the Buddha, nor yet for humanists to forsake their objective abandonment of miracles and the supernatural, in order to acknowledge that the Power we live by is the most significant, universal element in our existence. Our dependence on this Power must be evident to all of us. First we are dependent within our mother's womb; but once the umbilical cord is cut we are under a kind of 'remote control' or rather our 'internal battery' is powered by the same source that maintains our mother's life. Every living being is daily recharged by this power that is not of our own making, but given, or loaned, while we have breath. This is the greatest miracle – the miracle of life itself. There is no need for miracles that change the course of nature. Many wonderful and extraordinary things happen in the world, but none of these seeming miracles involve the reversing of natural laws.

But how can 'natural laws' compensate for 'a loving God who cares for us' and is concerned with our day-to-day behaviour: surely ruthless nature is quite remote from our interests? I have suggested elsewhere that Nature is a power for good – abounding in energy and creativity, it is *for life.* There is no need to evoke supernatural beings to control it. True, there are natural disasters: volcanic eruptions, earthquakes, floods and hurricanes. But such events derive from the very abundance, exuberance and energy of Nature. It is always astir, but there is no malice in its manifestations. Even death is the inevitable corollary of the abundance of life. Nature is not just 'interested' or 'concerned' with its products, but it manifests *a primal urge to create and protect,* to mother us in fact. Jesus called this power 'Father'. Had he lived in a matriarchal society he might have called it 'Mother'. Like a good parent, this Power does not seek to control us. We are not puppets, but have free will to use the energy at our disposal as we choose.

In many ways the Power we live by would appear to be more friendly towards us than some of the supernatural Gods that man has conceived. Take these words attributed to the *Old Testament* God in the law book, *Leviticus, (26:14-39):*

If you do not listen to me, if you fail to keep all these commandments of mine, if you reject my statutes, if you spurn my judgements …then be sure that this is what I will do: I will bring upon you sudden terror, wasting disease, recurrent fever, and plagues that dim the sight and cause the appetite to fail. You shall sow your seed to no purpose, for your enemies shall eat the crop. I will set my face against you, and you shall be routed by your enemies. Those that hate you shall hound you on until you run when there is no pursuit.

But it doesn't end there. 'If after all this you do not listen to me,' he goes on, 'I will punish you seven times over for your sins' ...If they remain disobedient he punishes them seven times more; and if that isn't enough, seven times seven. Finally, the punishments include, among other things: 'Instead of meat you shall eat your sons and your daughters...I will pile your rotting carcasses on the rotting logs that were your idols, and I will spurn you...'

In 'God's' favour it must be said that most of the passages in *Leviticus* begin: 'The Lord spoke to Moses and said, Speak to the Israelites in these words...'so, (since there is no means of checking up on the process of communication involved!) actually only Moses or more likely the Levite lawgiver can finally be held responsible for the words cited.

Or take *Romans (2:8-9)* in the *New Testament:* '...for those who are governed by selfish ambition, who refuse obedience to the truth and take the wrong for their guide, there will be the fury of retribution. There will be grinding misery for every human being who is an evil-doer, for the Jew first and for the Greek also...'

Likewise, in the *Qur'an* in the chapter called 'The Forgiving One', Allah is said to say to the Unbelievers: 'This you shall suffer because you rejoiced in wickedness and led a wanton life. Enter the gates of Hell and stay therein for ever. Evil is the home of the arrogant.' And in the chapter entitled *Al Hajj* (The Pilgrimage): 'They who believe not shall have garments of fire fitted to them; boiling water shall be poured over their heads; their bowels shall be dissolved thereby, and also their skins; and they shall be beaten with maces of iron.' (XXII, 19-21)

There are, of course, many comforting passages in all three of the scriptures quoted. But 'X' – the Power we live by – doesn't make promises or threats; it simply keeps us going as long as it can. It is non-judgmental. It accepts all religions and none, because it is part of all beliefs. We cannot escape it, except by suicide; and very few people want to give it up. Most people will struggle with all sorts of hardships, illnesses and disasters rather than give life up. They will take unpleasant medicines, do exhausting exercises, or undergo painful surgical operations rather than let go of life. Whatever else one believes, whatever 'added baggage' in terms of dogmas one subscribes to, this eagerness for life seems to be paramount. If we love life, it seems to suggest that life loves us. Without trespassing into anthropomorphic explanation, we must recognise that love is inherent in the scheme of things, otherwise we would not be able to experience it. For the concept of love and the fact of love we are totally dependent on the Power we live by and when we are loving we draw entirely on that source and sustainer.

Reverence for life

'God' as the 'Power we live by' is evidently a pantheistic concept since such a power is everywhere, inherent in all religions and none without prejudice. It is also mystical, since we can apprehend it spiritually without necessarily understanding it or its origin. After a prolonged study of the world's major religions, Albert Schweitzer came to the conclusion that the keynote and highest common factor of all dogmas and beliefs is that Life is sacred, and deserves our reverence. 'True philosophy [he wrote] must start from the most immediate and comprehensive fact of consciousness, which says: "I am life which wills to live, in the midst of life which wills to live".' From this basis he developed 'a mysticism of ethical union' with the fact of *Being* at is centre. Schweitzer showed how our world-view and life-view could merge in the simple, practical and personal principle of *reverence for life*. It is clear that his concern was with the power we *all* live by, animals as well as humans. He demonstrated that it was *universal* in the following example: 'If I save an insect from the puddle, life has devoted itself to life, and the division of life against itself is got rid of.' This occurs 'Whenever my life devotes itself in any way to life.'

It is well known that Schweitzer gave up the potential prospect of a European career in music, medicine or philosophy in order to found a hospital in Lambarene and work as a doctor in the disease-ridden Equatorial forest of Belgian Congo. In this work, he said: 'I enjoy a feeling of refreshment which prevents me from pining away in the desert of life.' He showed that the principle of *reverence for life*, if adopted, can inform and direct our individual thoughts, behaviour and life-style. It is an inward recognition of the Power we live by and its presence in all life.

The importance of this personal inner presence can be readily found in the scriptures of the major religions. In the *New Testament*, for example, we find: 'The kingdom of god cometh not with observation: Neither shall they say, Lo here! or, lo there! For, behold, the kingdom of God is within you.' (*St Luke:* 17:20- 21*)*.

In the *Qur'an,* Allah is said to declare that he is 'nearer to man than the vein in his neck.' (Ch.50:16). Buddhism, in different times and places, has taken many forms, but always at its centre is the individual inward act of meditation – to lose oneself and become one with the universe. Serious meditation (either alone or in a group) is a very personal religious activity, involving one's whole concentration. Buddhists are encouraged to 'Be lamps unto yourselves. / Be your own reliance.' And 'Hold to the truth within yourselves / as to the only lamp'. The veneration of the many wonderfully constructed statues of the Buddha, often with a comforting smile, suggests a widespread affection for this bringer of enlightenment to the many; but in no way negates the essential inwardness of practicing Buddhists.

One way Zen Buddhism seeks to help the individual to pierce through to the essence of 'being', 'truth' or 'reality' is by riddles that defy language. This is rather similar to a common technique of Chinese Taoism. The aim is to disentangle ourselves and our insights from the patterns and pressures that language imposes on the world. As I have written elsewhere, while words are valuable 'bridges' to enable us to communicate and get from one idea or place to another:

> They can also be conceived of as 'cages' imprisoning our minds in assumptions and preconceptions over which our conscious minds have little control, and blinkering us against awareness of alternative interpretations of things. (*London Educational Review*, vol.3, no.1, Spring 1974, p.53)

Both Zen Buddhism and Taoism seek to promote enlightenment through an intuitive apprehension of the nature of things – to pierce through the crust of everyday custom and verbalization to a personal vision of life's essence.

The Jewish, pantheist philosopher, Spinoza, was perhaps reaching for the same principle when he concluded that, 'in order to make himself known to men, God can and need use neither words, nor miracles, nor any other created thing, but only Himself.' Immediate contact with the Power we live by is available to us all at a very personal level if we are prepared to centre down and admit its influence.

While religions promote communication and cooperation between groups and communities and encourage sympathetic concern for others, personal spirituality is a necessary ingredient in order to develop *empathy*. Empathy is an inward awareness of the joy or suffering of others – a true fellow feeling that interprets others' needs. Thus it facilitates the practical expression or an attitude of 'reverence for life' by means of appropriate sympathetic actions.

Interventionist or 'interfering' gods?

For some people the essence of a personal element in religious life is the belief that their God is prepared to intervene in the world, to bend the rules of nature if required, to monitor our individual sins and transgressions and to judge us. But it seems to me that the majority of people are able to judge themselves by the 'inner light' of conscience. Our conscience is possibly partly innate – even animals, cats and dogs for example, often show a kind of guilt or remorse by their gestures – but it develops mainly as a result of our shared social development, discovering what actions are *for* life and which behaviours are destructive and *against* the harmony of our common life.

As for miracles in response to my individual prayers and the prospect of a personal afterlife, I began to give up belief in these at about the age of eight when I officially gave up Father Christmas. (I had had my doubts about Father Christmas for two or three years but had not owned up to them for obvious reasons.) I didn't like to mention giving up the afterlife immediately for fear of disillusioning my parents. They were evidently nearer their exit date than I was and so it seemed to me that they were more in need of comfort from the possibilities offered by a place reserved in heaven. Miracles in general I rejected at about twelve soon after I took up with conjuring. The wonder of our natural world is so awe-inspiring that I regard the idea of subverting its rules by divine intervention as *sub*-natural rather than super-natural. My God is firmly rooted in the natural (already miraculous) order.

A god that answered individual prayers – requests from the farmer for rain and prayers from holidaymakers for sunshine, etc, would be a magician. Even if such a deity existed he would be put in an invidious position by countless contrary requests! But most people as they grow up realize that this kind of prayer is not practical. We can *hope* for rain or sunshine, etc, but it is a waste of time praying for it. It's best to water the garden or take an umbrella. Sigmund Freud said that 'religion is an attempt to get control over the sensory world'. This is true of primitive, but not mature religion. Mature prayer is primarily a means of getting control over *ourselves*.

Inwardness of X

Fortunately, the inwardness of the Power we live by makes it highly accessible to every individual person. Prayer is essentially a question of surrendering our ego and centering down to the deeper level of ourselves that is shared by all sentient beings. It is less dependent on words than upon attitudes: a question of readjustment to reality, of widening our sympathies, reducing our fears and anxieties, and of taking stock of our strengths and weaknesses. Gandhi spent a great deal of his time and energy in meditation. For him: 'Prayer is not asking. It is a longing of the soul. It is daily admission of one's weakness'. In relation to the mechanical reciting of formal prayers he observed that, 'it is better in prayer to have a heart without words than words without a heart.' (*Gandhi, Young India, 23.1.1930*). He clearly believed that listening to the 'still, small voice' within was more important than voicing requests. There is no doubt that Gandhi achieved a great deal in the real world as a result of his prayer and fasting. There was no magic involved: simply sincerity, deep concern to abide by truth and justice, and determination.

We are not all Gandhis, but most of us experience the need from time to time to stifle our *hubris*, to acknowledge our selfishness, to admit to our faults, to summon up forgiveness for slights we may have suffered, to give silent thanks for good fortune when it occurs, to acknowledge the beauty and abundance of the world, or to ask for inner strength to cope with pain or deprivation in times of misfortune. There are times when we need to be (to quote the title of a noteworthy book) 'in tune with the infinite'. Recognizing and centering down to the Power we live by makes this easy.

For some people these adjustments are best achieved in calm and solitary periods of meditation. Perhaps for many more the reassuring solidarity of a likeminded congregation is a valuable support. In churches, synagogues, mosques and temples the beauty, solemnity and generally relative permanence of the building helps to establish a feeling of security, timelessness and calm. And for many, the hearing and sharing in the linguistic beauty of established sacred liturgy is an uplifting experience, raising the spirits above the level of the humdrum activities of daily living.

But whether alone or in the company of like-minded worshippers, the ultimate value of prayer lies in communion with our own innermost truth. It is in conversation with our own share of the Power within us that we can access its universal presence, and 'listen'to the response from our better self. There is no external super-being, no Big Brother, spying on our thoughts or meditation, or judging us. We are performing a similar operation to that undertaken by Jesus, Mohammed, Siddhartha Gautama (who gave us Buddhism) and other spiritual seekers – communing at depth to find a meaning and solution appropriate to our own personal situation at our own time. We may be glad to resort to insights gained from their teaching, but we are not unquestionably bound by answers that were appropriate in the *Zeitgeist* of their lifetime. The Power we live by is contemporary as well as eternal; personal as well as universal. It is God with no favourites, yet accessible to all.

I must point out here perhaps that I naturally use the conventional word 'God' in my own prayers! My use of the term 'X' in this book is simply to remind myself and my reader that the word 'God' is a concept that represents the Power we live by yet which is at the same time an impenetrable mystery. When I pray (despite what Richard Dawkins might think) I would not say 'Our X which art in heaven...' nor 'Our Power that we live by...' nor yet 'Our law of gravity...'! But I happily use the word 'God'! Incidentally, I find that what is known as 'the Lord's Prayer', beginning 'Our Father which art in heaven...' is as extraordinarily apt today as it must have been when first uttered, so long as we recognize the symbolic and poetic nature of some of the terms employed and interpret them appropriately.

Farewell to the old man with a beard

Richard Dawkins quotes a survey answered by a number of intellectuals, Fellows of the Royal Society and US academicians. One of the propositions put to them was:

> I believe in a personal God, that is one who takes an interest in individuals, hears and answers prayers, is concerned with sin and transgressions, and passes judgement.' (v. Dawkins, pp101-2)

Evidently, no doubt to Dawkins' delight, only 12 of these intellectuals agreed with the proposition and 213 disagreed. I don't find this particularly surprising. In the first place the proposition conflates a number of components, and in the second place the factors concerned are not defined. No doubt the respondents interpreted the 'personal God' as the familiar old-man-with-a-beard figure. In which case, I would agree with them. But this is not the God I have been proposing – the Power we live by. God in this sense is not a person, although potentially highly personal. As to hearing and answering prayers, this God will not change the weather, nor will it bring success in an examination for someone who doesn't work for it! However, a person in tune with this Power may draw on hidden strength in order to work harder and deserve success. If he or she fails, the same Power can help them come to terms with their situation and maybe try again. Either way it will not snoop on our sins nor sit in judgement on them. It seems, however, that in a sort of way it *is* 'concerned' with our transgressions. I recognize that the word 'concerns' is anthropomorphic! But the fact remains that we (nearly) all of us develop a conscience, self-judging our behaviour; and the capacity to do this is necessarily charged by the Power we live by, since there is no other.

Some years ago a book was written entitled *Your God is Too Small* (Phillips, 1956). Its title was apt and its contents wisely criticized narrow, parochial and bigoted attitudes to divinity. However, in another sense, we can also say that in some ways God has become too cumbersome. The 'experts' profess to know too much about his/her/its nature and burden the concept with a heap of surplus 'baggage'. We know so little of the ultimate origin and 'purpose' of Life that all we can be absolutely sure of is its *power*. If we focus on this there is room for all religions and none to find common cause in reducing religious tribalism and the ultra-atheist contempt this has induced in concerned humanists. Richard Dawkins suggests that Albert Einstein shared his view, and quotes the following passage to give a flavour of Einstein's religion:

> I am a deeply religious nonbeliever... (Einstein says)... This is a new kind of religion... I have never imputed to Nature a purpose or a goal, or anything that could be understood as anthropomorphic. What I see in Nature is a magnificent structure that we can comprehend only very imperfectly, and that must fill a thinking person with a feeling of humility. This is a genuine religious feeling that has nothing to do with mysticism... The idea of a personal God is quite alien to me and seems even naïve.

I don't find anything objectionable in this. It shows respect for the natural order of things and a sense of humility in the face of our ignorance. The final sentence refers, I presume, to the kind of God that is regarded as a magnified 'person'. Later Dawkins refers to further words of Einstein:

> To sense that behind anything that can be experienced there is something that our mind cannot grasp and whose beauty and sublimity reaches us only indirectly and as a feeble reflection, this is religiousness. In this sense I am religious.

Dawkins himself agrees with this attitude. And so do I, except perhaps with the terms 'indirectly and as a feeble reflection', since I believe these apprehensions can be, and often are, direct and powerful.

Both Dawkins and Einstein share an 'unbounded admiration for the structure of the world so far as our science can reveal it.' I go along with this also, except that

I wonder why one has to stop at 'so far as our science can reveal it'? Why should we not admire the structure of the world including those mysterious aspects that have not yet been revealed by 'our science'? I can see that one can argue that one has no right to admire something one hasn't yet seen; but the unwillingness to admire the structure of the world *en bloc* (taking the mysteries yet to be revealed on trust) seems to me to be somewhat partisan. It suggests that somehow science is responsible for the structure of the world rather than *vice versa*: it seems to forget that 'the structure of the world' is responsible for us – including scientists.

Dawkins, despite his commendable leanings towards Spinoza and a kind of pantheism, seems to take an overly mechanical view of the world's workings. The result is a curious hostility to the idea of prayer. For example, he quotes Carl Sagan's reference to the apparent impossibility of 'natural religion' since... 'it does not make much sense to pray to the law of gravity.' Quoting Steven Weinberg, Dawkins writes: 'If you want to say "God is energy," then you can find God in a lump of coal.' To this I reply: 'Why say "God is energy" in the first place – the term is inadequate.' And why disparage the 'lump of coal'? You can find God in a *nutshell* when you recognize that its existence depends upon the same Power that gave us our own lives. And as for the scorned 'a lump of coal', only a soulless or ungrateful person could fail to appreciate the comforting warmth it gives out when it releases its store of ancient sunshine for us on a cold night.

Dawkins also shares Weinberg's complaints that people 'will find God wherever they look for him..."God is the ultimate" or "God is our better nature" or "God is the universe".' I don't find this too depressing. Someone said, 'if everyone is thinking the same thing, then no one is thinking.' Everyone has to find their own route towards the Truth. Even scientists don't agree about everything.

Dawkins concludes the opening chapter of *The God Delusion* with the sentence:

> The metaphorical or pantheistic God of the physicists is light years away from the interventionist, miracle-wreaking, thought-reading, sin-punishing, prayer-answering, God of the Bible, of priests, mullahs and rabbis, and of ordinary language. Deliberately to confuse the two is, in my opinion, as act of intellectual high treason.

The implication is that if we do not agree with one or more of the constituents conflated in this sentence then we should not use the word 'God' at all. But because a word has multiple uses, that is no reason to abandon it. We would have to jettison half the words in the English Dictionary if we adopted this principle. The word 'love', for example means many different things to different people, do we therefore scrap it? Even 'science' means different things to scientists and so-called Creationists! Should we therefore abandon the word 'science'?

I agree with many of the criticisms Dawkins raises against intolerant, tribal or bigoted religion, but I refuse to give up the word 'God'simply because it is often put to ill use. It is useful for summing up the wordy expression 'the Power we live by'. I hope that many people will adopt the simplified, dogma-free *conception* of the divinity that I am recommending, but I can't expect them to use the term 'the

Power we live by' in their prayers: the term 'God' is much more concise, personal and familiar.

CHAPTER TWELVE

Conclusion: 'X' as universal

We think of faith as a source of comfort and understanding but find our expressions of faith sowing division... We need to understand just how we got to this place, this land of warring factions and tribal hatreds. And we will need to remind ourselves, despite all our differences, just how much we share: common hopes, common dreams...
Barrack Obama: The Audacity of Hope, 2006

Everyone has the right to freedom of thought, conscience and religion; this right includes freedom to change his religion or belief, and freedom, either alone or in community with others and in public or private, to manifest his religion or belief in teaching, practice, worship and observance.
Universal Declaration of Human rights, Article 18, 1948

Since wars begin in the minds of men it is in the minds of men that the defences of peace must be constructed.
UNESCO Manifesto, 1945

Extinction or adjustment?

There is no doubt that our 21st century 'global community' is in crisis. Most people want peace and a degree of prosperity, yet we spend vast amounts of our resources killing each other and destroying each others' environments, and mostly in the name of national, tribal or religious interests. For what appear to be the highest of motives, each generation bequeaths a legacy of disaster and prejudice to the next. How can we break this vicious circle?

All too often when nations or tribes think they are serving Allah or the Christian God, they are in fact serving Moloch or Mars, gods of sacrifice and war. In seeking simply to sacrifice themselves loyally to their gods, they end up by sacrificing thousands of others with them, either directly or as so-called 'collateral damage'.

In addition to the violent clashes between antagonistic religious beliefs; we are all faced today – whatever our beliefs – with a belated battle to reverse the effects of global warming and other environmental damage resulting from reckless plundering of the earth's resources. In view of the ensuing crisis, it is not surprising that a number of concerned scientific atheists feel obliged to mount an attack on religion in general. The hypocritical 'War on Terror' by nominally 'Christian' western powers without the support of the United Nations and the misguided behaviour of fundamentalist 'Muslim' fanatics who try to blow themselves straight up to paradise with high explosives has sullied the reputation of their more reasonable co-religionists.

Clearly, anachronistic religious behaviour that refuses to recognise the vast changes in our world, particularly in the last two or three centuries, is a significant feature endangering international understanding and peace. The Power we live by 'X' is universal, not tribal. It is responsible for every single creature, human and otherwise. It is high time for religions of every persuasion to adjust to the twenty-first century *Zeitgeist*. Unless we can abolish, or at least substantially reduce, religious and national tribalism there is very little hope for the future of civilized humanity.

Interestingly, the current environmental crisis centres geographically in the Middle East where religious differences are most acute and where cooperation for the limited residue of fossil fuels heightens the tension. Oil that has hitherto provided most of the energy for 'modernisation' is set to peak in the near future and then diminish. Ironically this key area, often regarded as 'the cradle of civilization', could well become 'the grave of civilization' unless international 'tribalism' can give way to common sense. Perhaps what has been called the 'Arab Spring' – an upsurge of democratic feeling in the Middle East is a reason – even though a fragile reason – for hope that desirable changes may eventually come about.

Meanwhile, the well-meaning debate between protagonists for and against religious faith in general seems to be creating more heat than light. If we are to cope successfully with our shared environmental crisis we also need to put aside religious and secular differences and cooperate globally.

Universality of the power we live by
The irony of the situation is that all the parties involved *do* share a common factor – a respect for the Power we live by. It underlies all the religions, and is studied in minute detail by scientists. Physicists try to unravel it by experiments; the

faithful pray to it under various names and try to define it by language – creating (respectively) their paradigms and dogmas in the process. But finally this Power – X – remains a mystery.

When Einstein said 'science without religion is lame; religion without science is blind' he was not talking about supernatural religion, but about natural religion, much in the way that Spinoza or Marcus Aurelius would use the term. But it doesn't need much imagination to understand what Einstein meant: that there is more to life than facts and material concerns. There is no absolute division between scientists and religious believers. Most European Christians accept the theory of Evolution without difficulty, and many scientists have religious sympathies or beliefs. Intelligent religion and intelligent science both avoid exclusiveness; have a concern for creating harmony; and share a desire to take on our global responsibilities.

Barack Obama describes how his mother's scientific study of anthropology in no way decreased her spirituality:

> In our household the Bible, the Koran and the Bhagavad Gita sat on the shelf alongside books of Greek and Norse and African mythology...[She] viewed religion through the eyes of the anthropologist that she was to become...and yet for all her professed secularism, my mother was the most spiritually awakened person that I've ever known.
> (*The Audacity of Hope,* 2006)

Clearly, contrary perhaps to some faith holders' expectations, rational thinking can enrich rather than undermine spirituality. So, too, can widening our understanding of alternative faiths and philosophies.

Gandhi's embracing of aspects of Christianity and Islam along with his original Hinduism, for example, was part of his objective search for Truth, and certainly deepened his spirituality.

Now more than ever we need to recognize the value of Albert Schweitzer's principle of *'reverence for Life'*, which is simply another way of saying 'reverence for the Power we live by'. After an extensive study of the major world faiths Schweitzer came to the conclusion that this was the core element underlying all religion and morality. Today, Schweitzer's dictum is highly relevant in two directions: first, it addresses our concern for humanity at large; and secondly it embraces our ecological and environmental concerns. *Reverence for life* as exemplified in the *Universal Declaration of Human Rights* provides us with a moral basis to guide us through the first of these issues. As for the second, Schweitzer's principle points to a renewed concern for nature – cherishing it for itself and for future generations, rather than despoiling it.

X and Language
There is an urgent need for our education systems – particularly in the Christian, Islamic and Hindu world – to inculcate some understanding of how language and our anthropomorphic tendencies influence our beliefs. The faithful could be guided to a better understanding of the origin and nature of the doctrines they affirm, and learn to interpret with more insight the poetic language involved in scripture. Apart from conflict between opposing religions, even within the context of the various faiths failure to interpret sacred texts tends to provoke sectarian hostilities.

Within the Christian context the Bible has undergone many changes partly to keep up with changing language and partly to distinguish Protestant from Catholic versions. In early seventeenth century England, the Roman Catholic 'Gunpowder Plot' as well as perpetual conflict between High Church and 'Puritan' Protestants were undermining social cohesion. In an attempt to bring about some religious stability King James 1 summoned a meeting of Church leaders to the council chamber of Hampton Court Palace. Wisely, a Dr John Reynolds calmed down the king's verbal attack on the Puritan representatives by suggesting that disputes arose because the current version of the Bible was 'corrupt and not answerable to the truth of the Original' and that it was high time for a new translation.

For six years 54 leading scholars worked on a new version. The beautiful language of this text has been an inspiration to many, but for some readers today its archaisms may be a barrier to understanding. In addition, its presentation, following tradition, in my view belies the nature of the material. From the 13th century the Bible has been divided into chapters for ease of reference, and from the 16th century it was further subdivided into verses. An unfortunate result of this is to turn the scriptures into a kind of textbook, so that the fact that the material is essentially literature tends to be forgotten.

There are many modern translations and adaptations of the Bible (see Sources), but my own preference, which might appeal to secular Darwinists as much as to the devout, is *The Bible Designed to be Read as Literature* (Heinemann, 1936). Printed without the paraphernalia of chapter and verse numbers every few lines, it facilitates the reader's appreciation of the beauty of some of the highlights of scriptural poetry and narrative.

Since God – X – is ultimately a mystery, the language used to express religious ideas is designed to appeal to the imagination, inevitably using poetry and symbolism Science, on the other hand, generally avoids rhetorical devices and concentrates on factual investigation and reporting. By this means it has achieved wonderful advances in technology, medicine, etc, and at the same time enabled us to break the bonds of superstition that clouded man's early attempts to understand the world. As a result many people now recognize that features such as angels, demons, paradise and hell are imaginative, poetic creations relating to our hopes, fears and emotions generally and are not facts of life. We know that miracles *against the natural order* do not happen. But we also know that there is a spiritual world, or at least a spiritual *attitude* available within all of us, which enables us to experience life, human relations and the environment more richly. It is possible to ignore or denigrate the Power we live by, but it is not possible (except by death) to escape it. More importantly it is possible to engage with it, at our deepest level, and to draw strength from it.

When we realise that language is changing and evolving all the time and that the transmission of historical documents – including facts, myths, legends and doctrines – usually involves the additional vicissitudes of translation, we tend to become less dogmatic and more receptive to new insights. We realise that seers and prophets addressing another age with other problems and priorities may not have meant exactly what they seem to mean today. John

Scupham, the first Controller of Educational Broadcasting for the BBC, put the problem clearly when he wrote that

> words are a slippery and indeterminate means of communication with obvious limitations'. They are 'the private instruments with which we build our private worlds (and) the public instruments with which we try to share them.' [Moreover – and this is the crunch –] 'It is only possible to communicate in words on the basis of shared experience as well as a shared language.
> (*Broadcasting and the Community, 1967*).

Since our religions and concepts of God come to us from societies and tribes living in vastly different circumstances from our own, in many cases up to several thousand years ago, it is not surprising that numerous inconsistencies and ambiguities will divide us. We need to have faith not so much in the absolute accuracy of the recorded details of what the founders did and said as in the spirit of the accounts. It is the sincerity, courage and integrity of the religious prophets and leaders – including Buddha, Moses, Jesus, Muhammad, and more recently Martin Luther King, Mahatma Gandhi and others – that demand our respect and reverence, even if we do not agree with every detail of their utterances, which may in any case not have had exactly the same meaning at the time they were offered as they have today. As St Paul wrote in his letter to the newly converted Christians in Corinth:

> Such qualification as we have comes from God; it is he who has qualified us to dispense his new covenant – a covenant expressed not in a written document, but in a spiritual bond;

for the written law condemns to death, but the Spirit gives life. *(NEB, II Corinthian: 3:4)*

Anthropomorphic confusion

The human mind thinks inevitably by means of human language, so it is only natural that mankind has constructed most of its 'gods' in human terms and visualizes them by means of human images. (Even in what appear to be exceptions such as the Hindu elephant god it is the humanized elements rather than the animal features that are prioritised.) Since we tend to make gods in our own image, it is not surprising that they sometimes appear to let us down. The rain doesn't come to water the needed harvest despite the prayers of the faithful. The good man dies young and the villain enjoys a ripe old age. Earthquakes, volcanoes and tsunamis destroy whole innocent communities, and so on... If we make gods in our own image we cannot blame them for not coming up to scratch.

But the mysterious Power we live by – X – lies deeper than human description can reach. It cannot be blamed for not providing what it has never promised. But it can be revered and respected for giving us life and for the reliability of its laws. More and more we are discovering how these laws work. Little by little we find that weather forecasts are getting more and more reliable. We know the causes of thunder and lightning, of earthquakes and tsunamis, and we know that they are not reprimands for our sins. We know that comets, eclipses of the sun and other heavenly manifestations are not portents of events to come. We know that certain plants and medicines can allay or cure our illnesses. Science reveals these truths little by little. But science is not a god: science achieves its goals through paying respect and giving detailed attention to the Power we live by.

Morality, tolerance and intelligent religion

Since we have all been produced by the same Power, there is nothing to suggest that our individual lives are differently valued by that Power. Beneath the uneven distribution of wealth, honours, clothing and life-styles that colour our different lives we are learning to recognise that our intrinsic value as human beings should be regarded as equal. The *Universal Declaration of Human Rights*, promoted after the horrors and devastation of World War II, recognises 'the inherent dignity and…the equal and inalienable rights of all members of the human family' as 'the foundation of freedom, justice and peace in the world'. Although the implementation of this accord has far to go (particularly in respect of women) it remains a landmark agreement for an international basis of morality.

The concept of equality embraces and implies the application of the Golden Rule: 'Do to others as you would have them do to you'. If we add to this principle the injunction that 'means and ends should be compatible' or that 'means should be regarded as ends in themselves' we have the basis for a sound moral code. It would outlaw such injustices as the torture perpetrated in the name of the so-called 'War on Terror' in the prisons of Guantanamo Bay and Abu Graib on the one hand and the excision or the 'honour' killings of women in certain extreme Islamist environments on the other. War in general, and the stockpiling and threat of nuclear weapons in particular, would be judged immoral. And if 'God' is understood as the Power we live by, warranting our respect and reverence, then nuclear war (possibly the Armageddon that some Christian groups aspire to before a Day Judgement in their favour?) would be recognised as the ultimate blasphemy.

This brings us to another moral issue. The Power we live by is the power we experience everyday in *this* world. Now that we understand how language and human imagination work, there is no reason to suppose that there is another world superimposed somewhere above (or below) this one to which entry is gained after a special Day of Judgement. Personal life after death can neither be proved nor disproved: but life *before* death doesn't have to be proved, it is self-evident. And it is this daily life on earth to which we should give our energies. There is plenty of room for improving the lot of thousands who are starving or live at the mercy of unjust laws and corruption.

Heaven and Hell are best regarded not as future prizes and punishments to be earned in the here and now but as states of mind existing in this world. Perhaps it is pardonable that Heaven and Hell have long featured as real 'places' in some religions: they seemed valuable as the 'stick and carrot' of morality – encouraging good behaviour and discouraging sin. But they have no place in mature religion. We have outgrown this mistaken principle of 'the ends justifying the means'. Good actions are their own reward; evil is (ultimately) self-destructive. We are judged every day by our lives in the present – by whether we use the Power we live by – X – in just and loving ways, or squander it destructively.

Application of the principle of equality leads inevitably to the increase of mutual tolerance. We cannot say that all religions and philosophies are equally good or bad. We can be mistaken about 'facts' let alone about absolute 'truth'.

Our individual knowledge about ultimate Truth is necessarily relative since our judgements are inevitable coloured by our own life experience. So it is unwise to declare that our own faith or outlook is the only valid one, or the best, and to decry all the others. Tolerance is not just 'putting up with'the views of others, nor does it require us to agree with the others'views. However, our acquaintance with and genuine effort to understand other religions or beliefs can benefit both parties. It can cement relationships with others: help us to clarify and understand our own faith better and lead to acquiring a less dogmatic and more spiritual religion. The world needs more tolerance and mutual understanding. Although our individual circum-stances differ, we are all in the same boat, after all.

Personal religion and X

Anyone who has travelled widely and had dealings with a wide range of people with different religions knows that you cannot judge a person by their religion. Among Buddhists, Christians, Jews, Muslims and every other persuasion you can find both exemplary individuals and villains, and every degree of vice and virtue between these extremes. The fact is that each person tends to find in their religion those elements that match with their inner compulsion. In general those who have been brought up in a secure environment by parents or guardians who are loving, just and reliable will tend to find in their religion (or secular philosophy) those texts, principles and customs that accord with that upbringing. The products of violent, unjust and capricious parenting may tend to be drawn to texts justifying similar anti-social personal expression. The scriptures can be read in a hundred different ways to satisfy personal impulses. This is why anchoring one's faith to the core element – X – the *Power we live by*, reinforced with Schweitzer's principle of *Reverence for Life* and the *Golden Rule* can help individuals to make right choices within the options of their given or chosen faith.

I hope that I have been able to show that God as 'X' – the Power we live by – favours rather than hinders *personal* religion since we all share immediate, individual access to this Power. It is both universal and highly individual.

Conclusion

By now it should be clear that I don't agree with Richard Dawkins that we should abandon the word 'God'. However, I believe that his criticism of religions in *The God Delusion* is a valuable wake-up call to the faithful in their churches, mosques and temples. We all need to get our acts together and bring them up to date. If we don't, secular society will become increasingly materialistic and cynical, and the churches and mosques will retrench more and more into tribalism and mutual hostility. The ecumenical movement has done much to bring contentious Christian divisions closer together and the World Council of Faiths and similar ventures are working to extend this kind of rapprochement to different religions. It is to be hoped that exchanging and modifying religious insights will encourage a deeper level of spiritual understanding between faiths and also reduce the gap between humanists and those professing a religious faith. Both are concerned with the search for truth, and there is often more overlap in the thinking of the two camps than is recognized.

The main cause of the current debate derives from the excesses on all sides of the argument. From the religious angle the denial of the principle of evolution, for example, is comparable to the blindness of the 'flat earth' believers or the Inquisitors who hounded Copernicus and Galileo. On the other hand, on the atheist side, Richard Dawkins' criticism has two weaknesses. The first is the one-sidedness of his attack on religion, which overlooks an abundance of charitable activity and personal sacrifice, social support and community activities, and on the aesthetic side a wealth of beautiful creativity in music, art, poetry and architecture for example. Secondly, he seems to think that religion will simply go away if the faithful are shown their errors. This is the *Dawkins' Delusion*. Religion has a deep hold on mankind.

Barack Obama pointed out in *The Audacity of Hope*, 'according to most recent surveys, 95% of Americans believe in God, and more than two-thirds belong to a church. 37% call themselves committed Christians, and substantially more people believe in angels than believe in evolution...Books proclaiming the end of days sell millions of copies...' Elsewhere, since the demise of most of the 'Communist Empire', religion is burgeoning in ex-communist countries. Islam, Hinduism, Judaism, Sikhism and Buddhism show no particular signs of decline, though there is a growing interest in reform within Islam and Christianity. All these religions are fulfilling a human need. Maybe they are not always fulfilling that need in the best way. There is always the possibility of bigotry and fanaticism bringing out the worst in some of the faithful; but these are the failings not the strengths of the institutions in question.

I hope that readers will by now realise why I have designated God 'the X factor'. This is as close as I can get to 'God in a Nutshell' – a vital mystery, shorn of all the linguistic, doctrinal and poetic accretions that tend to cause hostility between members of different faiths. A concept such as divinity is very hard to grapple with. Neither you nor I can define in detail the nature of the Power we live by, but we both know that there is some mysterious force beyond ourselves that got us here and keeps us going. Science can tell us a great deal about natural forces at both micro and macro levels, but WHY we are here and how to make the best of it is another matter.

Finally, twenty-first century technology offers us new opportunities to overcome the limitations of our birth environment's cultural ethos. Although we inevitably grow up initially within a particular religious or ethical framework, there is no excuse now for us to fail to examine and consider other points of view and ways of thinking. At the touch of a button computers can focus on the principles and practices of practically every other religion. We can briefly get 'inside' a wide variety of Christian, Muslim or Atheist patterns of thought and belief. We don't have to agree with every aspect of Protestant, Catholic or Orthodox Christianity nor of particular Islamic, Buddhist, Taoist or Atheistic conceptions. But we are privileged to live in an age when we can sample different ways of understanding our world and empathise (if only briefly) with them. If we can't learn to understand each other, technology in another direction gives us the touch of other buttons that could destroy human society completely. The choice is ours.

It is to be hoped that the different faiths will adapt to meet today's demands, but they will not go away. We need a shift of focus. Perhaps we can learn to concentrate on what unites us – the mysterious Power we all live by – and put less emphasis on the details that divide us. In any case, it is not *that* people believe in God that creates problems, but *how* they believe in God. And finally it is how that belief influences their actions.

Sources quoted or consulted

ANDERSON, Erica (1965) *The Schweitzer Album,* Harper/London

AHMED, Akbar S (1995) *Living Islam,* BBC/London

AL-HUSSEIN, Lubna A (2009) *40 Coups de Fouet pour un Pantalon,* Plon/ Paris

ALI, Ayaan Hirsi (2008) *Infidel,* Simon and Schuster/London

ANDREWS, Rex (1967) *A Critical and Experimental Study of the Use and Effectiveness of Visual Aids in Religious Education. (Unpublished MPhil. Thesis)* Univ. of London Inst. of Educn.

ANDREWS, Rex (1974) *'Words and Worlds'* in *London Educational Review, Spring, Vol.3, No.1,* Inst. of Educn./UK

ANDREWS, Rex (1979) *Literature, Dogma and Education: a study of Matthew Arnold's later criticism and its educational implications for today. PhD. thesis,* Univ. of London I.of E.

ANDREWS, Rex (1994) *International Dimensions in the National Curriculum,* Trentham/UK

ARNOLD, Matthew (1873) *Literature and Dogma,* Smith, Elder/UK

ARMSTRONG, Karen (2005) *The Spiral Staircase,* Harper/London

AURELIUS, Marcus (1964) *Meditation*s, Penguin Classics/London

BATES, Ernest S. (Ed.) (s.d. 1950s) *The Bible Designed to be Read as Literature,* Heinemann/London

BLUE, Lionel (2010) *The Godseeker's Guide,* Continuum/UK

BONE, Edith (1966) *Seven Years Solitary,* Bruno Cassirer, Oxford

BONHOEFFER, D (1967) *Letters from Prison,* SCM Press/UK

BONHOEFFER, D (1965) *No Rusty Swords,* Collins/UK

BRONOWSKI, Jacob (1976) *The Ascent of Man,* BBC/London

BURKE, Carl (1967) *God is for Real, Man,* Fontana, UK

BUTLER, Bill (1979) *The Myth of the Hero,* Rider & Co/London

CALVIN, John (1536) *Institutes of Christian Religion III*

CHOPRA, Deepak (2000) *How to Know God,* Ryder/UK

COHEN, J M and M J (1993) *The Penguin Dictionary of XXth Century Quotations,* Penguin Books/London

COLSON, Rob et al (Ed.) (2012) *Space,* Dorling Kindersley/UK

The Book of Common Prayer, OUP, (s.d.)

CRYSTAL, David (1995) *The Cambridge Encyclopedia of Language,* Cambridge University Press, UK

DARWIN, Charles (2008) *Evolutionary Writings,* Oxford/UK

DARWIN, Charles (1948) *The Origin of Species,* Watts & Co/UK

DAWKINS, Richard (2006) *The God Delusion,* Bantam Press/UK

DESCARTES Rene (s.d.) *Discourse on Method and Metaphysical Meditations,* W Scott/UK

DE BOTTON, Alain (20120 *Religion for Atheists,* Penguin Books/UK

DE KAYZER, Carl (1992) *God Inc.,* Focus/Amsterdam,

DUNCAN, Ronald (Ed) (1983) *The Writings of Gandhi*, (Faber and Faber) Fontana/UK

DURKHEIM, Emile (1968) *The Elementary Forms of the Religious Life*, George Allen & Unwin/London

EAGLETON, Terry (2007) *The Meaning of Life*, Oxford/UK

EDWARDS, Chilperic (1934) *The World's Earliest Laws*, Watts & Co/UK

EINSTEIN, Albert (1950) *Out of my Later Years,* Philosophical Library, New York

EINSTEIN, Albert (1969), (Essay in) *I Believe,* Allen and Unwin/UK

KHOKAR, Ashish (2003) *Ganesha,* KGM International/ India

GIBBON, Edward (1962) *Decline and Fall of the Roman Empire,* Fawcett/NY

GOLLANCZ, Victor (Ed) (1950 *A Year of Grace*, Gollancz/London

GRENE, David (1988) *The History of Herodotus,* Univ. of Chicago Press/USA

GUILLAUME, Alfred (1971), *Islam*, Penguin/UK

HAMMERTON, J.A. (s.d.) *Outline of Great Books,* Amalgamated Press/London

HAMPSHIRE, Stuart (1951) *Spinoza,* Penguin/UK

HAWKING, Stephen (1988) *A Brief History of Time*, Bantam, UK

HAWKING, Stephen (2010) *The Grand Design*, Bantam, UK

HAYAKAWA, S I (1966) *Language in Thought and Action*, Harcourt, Bruce & World Inc./London

HEASTER, Duncan (2001) *Bible Basics,* Christadelphian Advancement Trust/UK

HICK, John (1977) *The Myth of God Incarnate,* SCM Press/UK

HITCHENS, Christopher (2007) *God is Not Great,* Atlantic Books/UK

HOBBES, Thomas (2008) *Leviathan,* Oxford World Classics

The Holy Bible, Revised Version, Oxford/Cambridge, 1891 (1611)

HUSEIN, Ed (2007) *The Islamist,* Penguin Books/UK

HUXLEY, Julian (1933) *Essays of a Biologist,* Knopf/NY

HUXLEY, T H (1893) *Science and Hebrew Tradition,* Macmillan/UK

JAMES, William (1901) *The Varieties of Religious Experience,* Fontana/UK

KEEN, Sam (1986) *Faces of the Enemy,* Harper and Row/NY

KRAUSS, M (2012) *A Universe from Nothing,* Simon and Schuster/UK

KUNG, Hans (2010) W*hat I Believe* (*Trans.* John Bowden), Continuum/UK

LACEY, Rob (2003) *The Word on the Street,* Zondervan/USA

LEMU, B Aisha (1976) *A Student's Guide to Islam,* Macmillan Education,/UK

LOCKE, John (1948) *Essay Concerning Human Understanding,* Dent/London,

MASCARO, Juan (transl.) (1972) *The Bhagavad Gita,* Penguin/UK

MASCARO, Juan (transl.) (1965) *The Upanishads,* Penguin/UK

MAUGHAM, Somerset (1938) *The Summing Up,* Heinemann/UK

McGRATH, Alister (2011) *Why God Won't Go Away,* SPCK/UK

MILL, J S (1910) *Utilitarianism, Liberty and Representative Government,* Dent/UK

The New English Bible, Old Testament (1970) Oxford/Cambridge

The New English Bible, New Testament (1961) Oxford/Cambridge

Oxford Reference English Dictionary, (2nd Edition, 1996)

NEIL, William (Ed.) (1959) *The Bible Companion,* Skeffington & Son/UK

OBAMA, Barack (2008) *The Audacity of Hope,* Canongate Books/UK

PAREKH, Bhikhu (2008) *'Gandhi in the 21st Century'* in *The Gandhi Way,* No.94/UK

PHILLIPS, J B (1958) *Your God* is *Too Small,* Epworth Press/UK   PHILLIPS, J B (1952) *The Gospels in Modern English,* Fontana/UK

PINTO, Vivian de Sola (1969) *The City that Shone,* Hutchinson/UK

POPE, Alexander (1950) 'An Essay on Man', in *Penguin Poets* (ed. D Grant),

The Qur'an (various Translations)

DAWARD, N J (1966) Penguin Books/UK

ALI, Abdullah Yusuf, (2008) Tahrike Tarsile Qur'an Inc,NY

AL-ISLAMI, Al-Muntada (2004) Saheeh International/UK

M H Shakir (1988)Tahrike Tarsile Qur'an Inc./NY

RENAN, Ernest (1927) *The Life of Jesus,* Modern Library/New York

RHYS, Ernest (1915) *British Orations,* J.M. Dent and Sons/London

RUSHIE, Salman (1988) *The Satanic Verses,* Viking/UK

RUSSELL, Bertrand (1955) *History of Western Philosophy*, Allen and Unwin /UK

SACKS, Jonathan (2003) *The Dignity of Difference,* Continuum/UK

SAGAN, Carl, (1995) *Pale Blue Dot*, Headline/London

SCUPHAM, John (1967) *Broadcasting and the Community*, Watts/UK

SCHMIDT, F.W. (1912) *The Origin of the Idea of God,* Rowan and Littlefield

SCHWEITZER, Albert (1955) *My Life and Thought*, Guild Books/UK

SMART, Ninian (1995) *The World's Religions*, Camb. Univ. Press/UK

SMART, Ninian (1969) *The Religious Experience of Mankind,* Collins/UK

SPINOZA, Baruch (1930) *The Ethics of Spinoza,* J M Dent/UK

TAGORE, Rabindranath (1970) *The Religion of Man*, Unwin/UK

WEINBERG, Steven (1993) *Dreams of a Final Theory*, Vintage/UK

WILLIAMS, Rowan (2010) *Tokens of Trust*, Westminster, John Knox Press/UK

YOUNG, William Paul (2008) *The Shack*, Hodder & Staughton/UK

(Ed. Anon.) (1945) *British Orations,* Dent, Everyman's Library/UK [v. also T*he Message Bible* (2003) available on line]

Journals

The Week, The Gandhi Way, The Guardian. Independent, etc.

Afterword

God in a nutshell:
a reciprocal relationship

We live by a Power not of our own making.

All religions appear to acknowledge this Power.

We are both *subject to* the Power, and *empowered* by it.

The endeavour to understand the Power we live by is science.

Respect for it, by observing the Golden Rule, is ethics.

Reverence for the Power we live by is religion.

Endpiece

Writing a book about God is a bit like balancing on a tightrope. I know that I can't offend God. The wonderful and mysterious Power that we live by is above and beyond taking offence. But I realise that whichever way I lean I am bound to offend *someone.* As a species, however open minded we try to be, we tend to be creatures of habit in our thinking as well as our behaviour. We each have our own ideas about the deity (or in some cases about its non-existence) and we may feel aggrieved when someone appears to attack our deeply felt beliefs. I can only say that I have had no intention of hurting anyone's feelings, and if I have hurt yours I apologise.

In a court of law we are obliged to tell 'the Truth, the whole Truth and nothing but the Truth'. But in the occult world of spiritual belief, we cannot be a hundred per cent certain that our personal truth is the ultimate Truth. I can only tell you *my* truth and hope it makes some sense to you. If we ever meet, I will be happy to listen to *your* truth, and I might even be prepared to let mine budge a little as a result of our encounter! Though I have to admit that I've been a very long time arriving at the conclusions I have outlined, and in their latest form they are enmeshed in a great deal of detail culled from a wider range of sources and encounters than I've been able to mention here.

The more I think about the vastness of the universe and the limitless stretch of eternity, the more I feel the importance of the nature of our own contribution to the little patch of space and time allotted to us. Although I don't anticipate a personal afterlife myself, I respect the thinking of others for whom this is an important part of their belief. In any case, I am quite certain that we each contribute something of ourselves to the eternal stream of life; and it matters very much whether that something is life-enhancing or destructive. Whatever our beliefs about God may be, we have a responsibility to ensure that our acts are as far as possible contributing to a natural, political, social and spiritual environment that is as safe and friendly as possible for our grandchildren and their grandchildren as long as our small but precious world continues to spin on its axis.